*Everything is Politics but Politics
is not Everything*

Everything is Politics but Politics is not Everything

A theological perspective on faith and politics

H.M. KUITERT

WILLIAM B. EERDMANS PUBLISHING COMPANY
GRAND RAPIDS

First published in English 1986 by SCM Press Ltd, England

This edition published through special arrangement with SCM by Wm. B. Eerdmans Publishing Company, 255 Jefferson S.E., Grand Rapids, Mich. 49503

Library of Congress Cataloging-in-Publication Data

Kuitert, H. M. (H. Martinus), 1924-
  Everything is politics but politics is not everything.

  Translation of : Alles is politiek maar politiek is niet alles.
  1. Christianity and politics. I. Title.
BR115.P7K7913   1986   261.7   86-11586

ISBN 0-8028-0235-4

Contents

Introduction

1. What is this book about? A standpoint

This book has a standpoint. Anyone who is interested only in that can begin at chapter 15 and miss out the previous chapters, because the standpoint is indicated there. I may as well also point it out here, to spare the reader even more trouble. What I argue in this book is that the healthy discovery of the 1960s, that church, faith and theology also have a political side, has come to grief by being pressed too far, and has left Christianity in confusion. Everything is politics – that may be true; but at the same time politics is not everything. People, including the Christian churches and their members, need gradually to become aware of that again. The time is coming when they will note with regret that they have backed the wrong horse and made a mess of the Christian enterprise. I have written this book in order to cushion these people and churches against that time. I hope I shall succeed. That, put as briefly as possible, is my standpoint.

If I am to express it at somewhat greater length, then first of all I must say something about the basic presupposition of this standpoint. In fact, this presupposition is the state of affairs of the last ten or twenty years: politics has seized hold of the church, church discussion, church preaching, church catechetics and (church) theology. For years political preaching was a hot item; now it is ebbing away. I see this as an indication of uncertainty over the way things have gone. Instead there is vigorous discussion about political theology. Is there less uncertainty about that? It will not be my fault if I raise a number of questions in this book which at any rate stimulate reflection here. As a background accompaniment you will also hear the slogan that faith has always been 'utterly political' (Karl Barth) so that we are completely wrong if we separate faith and politics. Now I am not going to do that either; faith and politics are inseparable, nor have I separated them anywhere. But in 'not separating' them I have not yet said anything about how we must combine them, and it may well appear that at this point there are pitfalls and traps which may make theologians and church people stumble. At the appropriate place I shall go into this in more detail.

Here I am content to illuminate my position. 'The church must make political statements', 'theology is only relevant if it is political theology', are standpoints which I do not share. So everything is politics? Very well, let us assume for the moment that Christianity is not persuaded of that and has not been tricked out of making its own contribution – by going down that road – what does that mean? Those who use the slogan mean that even something which you find to be of no concern to another grouping (for example, the state), is nevertheless part of the power struggle over the realization of ideals. That seems right to me. Even 'not everything must be politics' is in this way a contribution to the political struggle. But is politics everything that goes on in the world? Christians must know better and must do both politics and the Christian church a service by saying fearlessly that they know better. Politics and the church lose their natures if everything becomes politics. To stick to the churches in my country, the Netherlands: in that case the Christian religion becomes a religion of activists. Sometimes these activists are (still) optimists, who have seen the glimmering horizon of the kingdom of God light up in their own political ideals and will not tolerate any delay, but some are also pessimists who have begun to despair of their own ideals and therefore preach all the more fanatically that no matter what, the kingdom must come and that Christianity is involved with believing the impossible. But faith, at least Christian faith, is not frustrating, however much misery people can also experience with God. People frustrate themselves and fob off on God or others the frustrations that they feel. There is more to Christian faith than action.

There is also much more in it than believing that our action will result in the world being saved from the catastrophe of a nuclear war or an ecological disaster. If that is all that Christians believe, they would do better to shut their churches immediately, since such a faith has nothing to offer the church or the world but exaggerated self-importance and fanaticism. Such a reduction of faith can be the result of naivety – anyone who comes into contact with politics for the first time finds a new world opening (which then closes again) – but I am not completely certain of that. Politics always involves a power struggle, as I shall demonstrate in due course. It would not be surprising if it should subsequently transpire that the church and religion – yet again – had been a weapon in the struggle in which a new élite tried to dispossess an old one. But that too could be a fight that was undertaken in all naivety.

In saying all this I am not doing down action; that much should be clear. Nor am I (least of all) doing down action at the level of political and social regulations. I am more concerned to restore its proper proportions, at least the proportions which it has for Christian faith. That is my standpoint – again – but now I am indicating it to the non-Christians who read this book. The discussion in this book will be as rational as possible, since that is what theology should be: anyone who does his or her best and is interested in it must be able to follow it, but that does not exclude adopting a standpoint, and that standpoint is that Christian faith does not go with a total politicization of human life. Let me make this as plain as I can: in writing *Everything is Politics but Politics is not Everything* I have had in mind our national situation, as we experience it every day, and the place of the church and faith in it. That certainly does not mean that the rest of the world is irrelevant to it, but the question of what political action might be best for Latin America or Black Africa – just to mention these two areas – is not one that I can solve here. So this book is about us; when it is otherwise I shall say so.

Now this book is not just an indication of my position over the politicization of the church and faith; it is also a theological analysis of the alternatives between which people have had to decide to have got so far. The greater part of the book is devoted to these theological analyses. How far can Christian faith be inflated politically without bursting like a balloon? That is the central theological question that I am raising here. I am concerned to answer it as precisely as possible. There will be no question of producing slogans and counter-slogans in the relevant chapters (those of Parts I-III); I hope, rather, that there will be meaningful and matter-of-fact theological arguments, which challenge everyone to reflect on them. I would be sorry if my adoption of a standpoint meant that the people whom I am particularly concerned to reach stopped reading. The reason why I began by declaring my own position was neither to provoke nor because I am eager to convert people, but to express a commitment. I do not want to be included in the ranks of theologians who write about theologians who write about theologians and so on. But what are the alternatives with which I am concerned? In order to help the reader, here I shall indicate them as they appear in each Part of this book and in the form of the conclusions that I draw.

What I assert in Part I amounts to the view that theology is not political theory, far less a criticism of society.

Part II has turned out to be quite long. In it I claim – as argumentatively as possible – that the truth and value of religious faith (and therefore also of Christian faith) are not determined by what political, social or other kinds of theories see in faith. Faith itself also has to say what its value is.

In Part III the theologians have pride of place. This Part ends with the statement that neither in theory nor in practice can one derive directives for action from eschatology – the doctrine of God's coming kingdom. Anyone who tries that lands in a dead end.

As to Part IV: Christians are active in politics for human well-being (if they do it well), but well-being is not the same thing as God's definitive salvation in which people share through Jesus Christ and his Spirit. The dead are not raised by politics. There is no political route to the messianic kingdom.

The last Part (V) asserts that the churches cannot act as political agents and that it is a good thing for them not to want to. Duplicating what others are doing (political parties and ideologies) amounts to halving oneself. We can also say that Christians always have twin roles, being members both of the Christian church and of society, and these roles do not run so smoothly into each other as right-wing Christians used to think and left-wing Christians now suppose.

As I have already said, these Parts will be about theology, but in the form of a discussion of the alternatives between which one has to choose before arriving at the politicizing of the church and theology. I have used the term alternatives with a particular image in mind: it presupposes junctions at which one can take different directions, but not all directions are worth recommending. I shall also point that out sometimes, but that is as far as I go here. It is not my concern to engage in polemic with particular theologians or to subject particular trends in theology to far-reaching analyses. That would make this book far too long. But above all, that was not my intention in writing it. I want to bring out the junctions in the discussion about faith and politics (it might be better to say the junctions that have been missed) on the basis of a particular interest. Therefore in each Part the screw is also tightened one turn further. I cannot feel that it is a good thing for church, faith and theology to be sacrificed on the altar of politics, since politics is not everything. Although a large number of people may still believe that, Christians do not. Sometimes faith consists in *not* believing what others believe.

Finally: the amount of reading matter on the subject is so great that I am not ashamed to confess that I have only skimmed the top of it. I must say that I have found writing this book more than usually difficult. That is partly because of the enormous amount of literature that I have already mentioned: I have been more than usually troubled over asking myself how I can make a good choice from it, what simplification is profitable and what is not, how cavalier one can be about leaving out material, what has to be left out and what put in. But there was yet another disturbing factor: can enough ever be done for those without rights, the poor, the exploited of our world? The answer is no. But one suggests that by any criticism of faith and politics, giving the impression of no longer being loyal to all those who work for others honestly and with great personal dedication.

Finally I got over that feeling. The first argument was that, while not enough can be done for others, it can be done wrongly, in the longer or the shorter term. The second argument was that I am setting out the facts with which we (Christians) must deal differently, not saying what we must do. Why? To a large degree because in my view liberation from poverty and oppression can be done much more simply than it seems to be done by the official so-called political theology; however, in that case it must be detached from theology. What one then loses is the affirmation that God wants it. And that no longer makes things so easy. What one gains is less tension, more consideration, among Christians, too, and as a result better opportunities for a consensus in political and social affairs.

So where it comes to words, I want to argue for the poor and the oppressed just as much as any political theologians: as a member of the church I am even more concerned because I am arguing for a non-political diaconate. But I mistrust politics through the church; that makes the churches lose their nature; as a result politics becomes devalued and it is not inconceivable that Christians socialize their faith. Both socially and politically faith becomes achieving the well-being of others. That is too little, too naive (often it remains at the verbal level) and also too risky. Political power and political combativeness are needed for the realization of any ideal whatsoever. It is unthinkable that Christians in their day should not be just as hungry for power as anyone else and not just as concerned as anyone else to achieve it. Politics seems to me to be the ideal place for fulfilling these needs; that is where personal ambition can have a collective use. In the churches things are different; there it comes to grief.

I A First Reconnaissance

2. *The difficulty of discussing politics*

Religion, politics and sex, as van Ruler said in one of his books, are the only subjects which are worth bothering about. I would add that they are at the same time subjects over which people find it difficult to disagree with one another in a peaceful way. That is clear from what actually happens: discussions about politics – for the moment let me leave it there – usually turn into heated debates without any useful effect worth mentioning; there is no agreement, no *rapprochement*. Discussions about faith and politics are usually even more difficult, although they are carried on by people who share the same faith.

Why is that, and can anything be done about it? Can things be different? I want to use this chapter to make a practical beginning. Many reasons and causes can be advanced as to why it is difficult for people to talk with one another. It is impossible to follow through all of them, and in any case I am not competent to do so. At all events, what I am going to do is rather different: to connect the difficulty of discussions about politics with politics itself and at least try to show that it is in the nature of things that differences of political opinion should have a violent outcome. But that is no reason for abandoning honest conversation or attempts at it. In its own way, this book is also one such attempt. It seeks to show that it is possible to speak peacefully and quietly about all kinds of themes which are connected with faith and politics and thus are also political by nature. It is even meant to be a contribution towards mutual conversation and encouraging others in their turn to make a contribution, without falling victims to the illusion that all the problems in the world can be solved by honest conversations. To argue for discussion can have a much simpler basis: as long as talking is going on there is no fighting.

Why are discussions about politics so difficult? Let me begin with a trivial reason which really has nothing to do with politics but can

affect all discussion: people often want to be right and not to engage
in real discussion at all. By discussion I mean convincing and being
convinced by new insights and arguments. Those who identify
themselves with the standpoint that they adopt do not want to have
any new insights. The more people identify themselves with the
views that they hold, the more they are out to be right and the less
they can tolerate the disagreement of others.

There can be more than one reason why people identify themselves with the standpoint that they proclaim, and do so so stubbornly
that they cannot be shifted from it. This may be connected with the
structure of their personalities: some people hold their own by
keeping to what they have said once they have said it. keeping to
what they said once. What I mean is that some people are difficult
to talk to not because of the subject under discussion but because
they are who they are. For others the discussion becomes difficult
precisely because of the subject matter. A person needs some
convictions more than others in order to keep his or her head above
water. If the convictions are attacked – first from outside and then
from within – then people become uncertain in an area in which
they cannot cope with uncertainty. Because their convictions have
been put at risk they have been put at risk, and the more they feel
like that, the less ready they are to put their conviction – literally –
to the test. They cannot risk not being right because they are their
standpoint.

Above all among the older generation, there are people who – to
give an example – are violently against cohabitation and cannot
have any open conversation with their children about it. That often
(though not always) means that the ease with which their children
behave at a sexual level has made parents unsettled about an attitude
which they have held – and needed – all their life: a particular view
of the connection between marriage and sexuality. If they allow
themselves to be dissuaded from their view they must begin to work
out the husband-wife relationship all over again, and people are not
very keen to do that if they have found difficulty in arriving at a
particular equilibrium. Indeed perhaps they find it impossible: an
old dog cannot learn new tricks.

Is it then wrong to want to keep your head above water when you
feel attacked? Of course not, but that need not relate to the way in
which you want to be right. However, I do not want to say that even

that is wrong: it usually just happens, whether we like it or not. But it certainly makes things difficult. Anyone who only wants to be right in a discussion – for whatever deep-seated reason – isolates himself or herself by becoming incapable of being a conversation partner, since to be a conversation partner it is at least necessary for you to give the other person as much credit as you want for yourself.

Is it then wrong to hold on to certainties? No. People cannot do without them. But not all certainties are as certain as we would like. That is already clear from the simple fact that feelings of uncertainty can hit us so hard. No positiveness, no vehemence, no overwhelming vote, not even being as right as you can imagine can help that. But why should we look for certainty in this particular direction? When there is every reason for feelings of uncertainty we can take a much better course: learn to live with them instead of running away from them. On the level of faith we know that everything is not as certain as our confidence might suggest. When it comes to politics, then we feel, as we shall see, even more in the dark. So on these premises, any conversation about faith and politics already begins with a complex handicap. There is no need for it to stifle the conversation if we can see how to make a virtue out of necessity by accepting that although we may be right – after all, this is the position from which we must start, though we may shift from it – our standpoint is not as unshakable as it might seem. Anyone who can accept that no longer needs to be so vehement.

To this 'acceptance' I would like to add something else. People must also accept one another, i.e. at least allow others to be themselves in their own right. People who speak sympathetically about feminists, progressives who sweep the floor with the conservative evangelicals, and those, of course, at the other extreme, will have already *a priori* frustrated discussion probably because they are threatened by considering their position as something that is open to discussion. In any discussion, what people need to do is let others be individuals in their own right. Christians are people, too, and are no different from others in that respect. What I have said so far applies to some degree to any discussion, and therefore also to political discussion. There is a second reason why discussions on the political level are so difficult. It is connected with the previous one. As we have seen, people often identify themselves with the standpoint that they take. It seems that they do that above all in politics: they are the political convictions that they cherish. How does that come about? First of all, a person needs a group (a group of people), since a group provides an identity. There he or she has a name, is known and recognized. People do not pursue politics on their own but in groups. By taking part in a political group they derive identity as political subjects. This group need not immediately be the political party of one's choice (or of one's father and mother), though that is often the case. We can also think of ideological trends in the political or social sphere.

Becoming involved in a political group – I am keeping to politics simply for convenience – provides identity, it makes me what I am. But how does one get involved in it? By having a political conviction, the one that the group holds. So perhaps it would be better to say that we become involved by approving a political conviction. Thus political identity and having or maintaining a conviction coincide. Compared with what I said earlier, that is a much more important cause of fierceness and irritation in political discussion. People all too easily feel that attacks on their political convictions and disputes about political ideals and directives are an attack on their own identity; they feel that they themselves are being put on trial. For what is political identity? To get a better understanding of that – and at the same time of the passion, the fierceness and partisan nature of political conversations – we must first go a bit more deeply into the phenomenon of politics. Another advantage of that is that I can establish right at the beginning of this book in what sense I use the word.

What is politics? It is impossible to outline the scholarly definitions which are currently in use. That would take too much space and time and would lead me far beyond my own competence. So I shall say what I understand by politics in the rest of this book and what – as far as I can see – truly corresponds with the current definitions. Above all, I shall show what makes it clear why political discussion can be so fierce and discouraging. Whenever I talk about politics – or use the adjective political – I shall presuppose that the term has two components: 1. ideals and 2. gaining power in order to realize those ideals. By ideals I understand both political and social ideals, in other words, an ideal organization of human relationships in the sphere of the distribution of power and an ideal organization of human relationships in the sphere of interests. So politics is a matter of human relationships: that is the first thing I would add. Political and social organization has an instrumental relationship to human beings as persons. I would also make a distinction between political and social, though social questions (work, family, man/woman relationships, distribution of income and so on) ultimately have political solutions. But this last point demonstrates again that society is not the same as politics, even if we take into account that the formation of power also happens in the social sphere. There is also economic power and social power. This sort of power can play a considerable role in the gaining of political power, but the converse is equally possible: that politics restricts or at least challenges this power.

So political discussions are about ideals which can only be achieved through the gaining of power. They are not just about ideals: that would be far too naive a definition of politics. Nor are they just about gaining power; politics is more than dealing with power because this power is used for something, otherwise it becomes incomprehensible why we do not find one power as good as another. Ideals and the power to realize those ideals together – as an indivisible whole – form what we call politics. What does that mean for political discussion?

Let us begin with visions and ideals: a person does not just become a supporter of a group; he or she supports that group through the choice of an ideal. He or she becomes identified with that ideal, with one of the many symbolic expressions of it, with the directives derived from it, and in so doing confirms his or her political (and social) identity. The more ideal an ideal is, the more identification there is and the less dissociation. We can now understand that better – and the vehemence which goes with it. But even that is not all. In politics people are no longer involved as idealists but as a social and political group. As Marx put it: human beings are a combination of their social and political roles. We shall return later to the question whether that is the whole person. Should that be the case, then one would have no other identity than a political or social identity. But as we shall see, a person is not just given identity by the group or society. He or she also has a religious faith and in addition to that is of a specific sex. A person need not just be a socialist or liberal; he or she can also be a child of God and additionally a husband, wife or partner to another.

But all that will come up later. Here we can accept that if we take these restrictions into account – the competing identities – individuals are also part of a social and political whole and therefore the ideas and ideals which they cherish about the distribution of power (politics) and the just distribution of obligations and rewards (society) also affect them and their own place in the whole. And not just themselves in their own particular place: we do not have a sense of injustice only when we ourselves are in trouble but also when we see that others are being treated unjustly, and a sense of injustice is a very powerful feeling. That also explains part of the emotion in political discussions. Part of it, but no more. It is impossible for someone to be involved in politics or social criticism and at the same time to ignore his or her place in the whole. He or she would soon cease to have a place and be eliminated as a political and social factor. What hold does he or she have on power as things are *now*, and what is the gain or loss if political circumstances change? And what becomes of one's own social interests if the social system favoured by others is implemented: is one then better off or worse? No one becomes a supporter of any political ideal or idea without these questions coming up. By becoming a supporter of a group or trend at the same time one becomes a supporter of oneself, one's own political role and one's own social interests. There is nothing wrong with this: one's own interests and Christian ethics are not mutually exclusive, as Manenschijn has demonstrated. Paying attention to one's own interests does not make one a conservative citizen. Why should being conservative coincide with being a conservative in the political sense? As soon as one has something – prestige, power, prosperity, not to mention love – one wants to keep it. Left-wing intellectuals also have their concerns, if it is only that everything that marks *them* out for prestige, power and prosperity disappears when all goes (too) well – as do the welfare workers! A partisan of the poor (the expression comes from Karl Barth) cannot be their partisan without the poor, just as of course a theology of the poor would get nowhere if there were no poor people.

However, even to note that by choosing a political and social ideal someone can put himself or herself socially and politically at stake is still not the whole story. It explains much of the fierceness and the difficulty, but not all. For that we must go back to the other element in politics. We should see this as comprising not only visions and ideals (by which a person indicates his or her position), but also the gaining of power to realize the ideals. Anyone who approves a political ideal approves a power struggle; anyone who is untrue to an ideal betrays the struggle for power. Therefore the political party or group cannot cope with dissidents. In the world of political ideals, orthodoxy prevails, as it used to prevail in the churches. We could well say that it prevails even more strongly, since deviation from Christian doctrine relates to God and the Christian churches finally accepted that this did not change God: he could take it. But deviation within a party or ideological trend relates to an ideal that must be realized and ideals are clearly much more shaky than God. Anyone who does not join in the realization of the ideal is a traitor. Moreover, when orthodoxy in politics becomes combined with orthodoxy in belief, for example in the requirement that Christians should be socialists if they are to be Christian, then orthodoxy is squared and political passion is multiplied by religious faith. That rules out discussion; all that is then possible is condemnation – presumably mutual.

So it is the factor of power and the gaining of power – indissolubly connected with politics – which infinitely frustrates political discussions. For we can say that one need not always want to be right, that we can learn to live with uncertainties, that identity need not merely be connected with the political role, but threatens power. A conversation partner is preoccupied with politics and thus with gaining power. In that case is not the other partner equally concerned with keeping (or gaining) power? That is probable, but it does not contradict what I am claiming here: because politics is politics, political discussions are mortgaged to the power struggle. So they are more difficult to carry on than any other discussion, and a place has to be found where people can talk with one another right outside the power struggle. I shall come back to that later.

Where there is no such place or people do not want to look for one, political conversation remains difficult and creates mutual mistrust and even anxiety. That seems to me not only to be unavoidable but also – from the perspective of self-defence – indispensable until the contrary emerges. Anxiety is a bad counsellor, but a touch of anxiety in politics is indispensable. If we had been rather more anxious in Western Europe about National Socialism we would have resisted it more – and as a result perhaps with more success and fewer victims. If people today are anxious about Soviet Communism, it seems to me that their anxiety is also justified – simply on the basis of the fact that more people were killed under Stalin than under Hitler. Moreover I do not see why Dorothee Sölle thinks that as a Christian you cannot be anti-Communist but may be a Communist. That seems to me to be not only logically untenable but also politically naive. Suspicion of *any* power is a necessary element of an adult political consciousness. I am not talking about the fact that such remarks are a very simplistic legitimation for political standpoints in terms of religious faith. I shall go into that problem – the problem of religious legitimation – in one of the subsequent chapters.

To return to the question with which we are concerned: political discussions are burdened with the question of gaining power. I have certainly exaggerated the problems involved. Discussion is not always so heated on every topic. People may be at loggerheads over their political views, but they can also be detached about them. That provides openings for conversation. And we must have conversation if we do not want power to decide everything and honest arguments no longer to count. Nevertheless, the dimension of gaining power makes it impossible to carry on conversation too naively. Naivety is not a gospel virtue. If Christians do not know how to combine it with the cunning of serpents, then they will sink along with their faith and everything else. Church, faith and theology offer excellent help to people who want power. All three have to do with God and anyone who has to do with God has to do with the supreme authority for believers. If we want to avoid the Christian faith being as easily tied up with the left as it was – at least in certain countries – with the right and for the umpteenth time entering a Babylonian captivity, then the least a theologian can do *qua* theologian is to clear up relevant questions or – to put it the other way round – to remove confusion. Where confusion arises, not only does political conversation come to grief but people, including church people, become an easy prey for manipulators. They also get involved in things that they do not intend, or things that they ought to do if they knew what they meant do not get done. So opposition to confusion and the smokescreens of scholarship and a continuing search for clear terminology has nothing to do with rationalism but with defence, with protecting people from becoming the victims of others.

There is certainly a problem here. Politics needs slogans, since slogans make people enthusiastic and enthusiastic people combine to become a power factor. So slogans are emotional but seldom clear. Anyone who looks for clarity and qualification is a wet blanket, slows down progress and is likely to be asked in a cold way for his or her credentials. Nothing can be done about that. There is a price to be paid for doing away with confusion. The confusion that I envisage in this context is the confusion of church, faith and theology. In the next chapters I shall be insisting that it has to be removed.

It was my aim to make a practical start with this chapter. So I shall end it with three practical questions which should really be raised by those who engage in discussions about politics: 1. Do I want only to be right? 2. Am I what my political conviction is? 3. Must others be on their guard because I am out to gain power?

3. Against confusion of languages

Discussions on politics can be frustrated not only by political passions but also by the simple fact that those who take part in them mean different things by the same words. If that is the case, for that reason alone the discussion ends in a hopeless tangle. The main aim of this new chapter is to try to disentangle the knot at least as far as terminology goes. I shall not do that by analysing what other people mean by words like church, faith and theology. That would be an endless task: whom would we include, whom would we exclude, and how could we cover everyone at all times? In a concern to explain what I myself mean by these terms, I shall of course come up against other views, but that is as far as I shall go. I think that I can best serve clarity by indicating what I myself mean by terms like faith, church and theology, as far as possible in connection with politics.

Faith and politics is not the same thing as church and politics, and that again is not the same thing as the combination of theology and politics. Of course the terms faith, church and theology overlap at particular points, but they are not interchangeable; at least they are not as interchangeable as the terms friendship, marriage and relationship, although these also overlap to some degree.

By theology I would understand a university discipline that needs to follow the rules of the scientific game if it is to have a legitimate place in the university. There are problems here as far as theology is concerned, no matter what direction we take, about God and his revelation and what can be said about these in scientific terms. I shall leave this question on one side for the moment and return to it later. All I am saying here is that the aim of theology of course takes this direction: it tests the truth-value of what people say about God and his salvation, so as to be able to express as accurately and as authentically as possible who God is and where we must look for him and find his salvation. Thus theology involves two things: testing what is said about God (for the moment I shall leave aside the criteria to be used here) and formulating or reformulating an outline proclamation, as is done in the theologies of, say, Bultmann, Barth or Boff. The accents can be placed at different ends of the spectrum at different times, but unless it does this testing theology is not worthy of its name and without an outline proclamation nothing can be tested. The theological perspective of this book – which is expressed in the sub-title – begins from the concept of theology formulated here. I want to test the truth-value and therefore the authenticity of what is said about God in the context of faith and politics (to put it in the most general terms). At the same time I am offering an outline proclamation which in turn needs testing – by others as well as myself.

This description of theology – academic testing and outline proclamation – opens one door and closes another. What is contained in an outline of proclamation by the Christian church depends on what a particular theologian thinks that it must contain. Justification by faith, the kingdom of God – it really depends on the theology in question how the outline is filled out. As long as this is not done in a completely arbitrary way there is nothing against it. In this respect theologians function as the opinion makers of Christianity. They are not right *a priori* – that is why I call it an outline proclamation – so there must be a test (which they must perform themselves) as to whether their assertions are tenable in the light of the Christian tradition. Remembering this can have a salutary effect. Theologians are not prophets, nor mediators, nor funnels from God (or to God) but earthly men and women who are all faced with the demand to say important things which means that they have produced a new outline proclamation. So politics can also have a place in a new outline proclamation. There is nothing against that. Theologians are quite free to include politics in their outline proclamation – of whatever kind. Then it is for us – again in all honesty – to say whether we find the outline tenable or untenable, catastrophic or productive, and why we arrive at such a verdict. What theology cannot do, in other words anything that does not involve an academic, professional discipline and outline proclamation, should not be done. However, there is an opening for it.

What theology cannot do – on the basis of the description that I have given – is be a theory of or for praxis, whatever people may mean by that. I must add that last comment, since it is usually unclear what theologians who use the term praxis – for example, Hellmut Gollwitzer – mean by it. It derives from the Marxist tradition and there it denotes a clarificatory theory which even explains (and thus predicts) the complete history of our society. It also denotes all the presuppositions which go with such a theory, including the presupposition that science can explain everything and that what it cannot explain is based on an illusion. Similarly it denotes that a scientific explanation is not only a description and an explanation but at the same time shows what people must (in the sense of ought to) do; in other words, it is descriptive and prescriptive.

It is hard to see how theologians can regard their own outline proclamation as such a positivistic theory. In that case do they mean by praxis what others mean? For example, in the case of Gollwitzer, a normative theory for action, a theory for political action? That could be, but in that case it is remarkable to call such a theory theology. In any case, it used to be called a programme of action for Christian politics. Questions may certainly be asked about the possibility of such a programme for Christian political action, though a century ago Christian politics was carried on with the help of such a programme. However, there must have been a reason why they never called it theology, a reason which I shall be giving in the course of this chapter, so that I shall not be discussing it here. For the moment it is enough to note that theology, if by that one means an outline proclamation, cannot be the theory for a practice unless by theory one means a normative theory for action. But in that case we get into a hopeless tangle over the term praxis. We must understand it to mean doing something. And in that case no theory without praxis means no faith without action. That is certainly true: believing without doing is not believing. But why must believing be called theory and doing praxis? Why is this praxis (this doing) so limited that it only envisages political action? Is that all that Christians do? I raise these questions simply to demonstrate the bewildering confusion in which we find ourselves through calling faith, theology or Christian teaching theory and (political) action praxis. Nor have I yet said anything about the view – which goes with this – that not only do theory and praxis form a unity but that theory is changed by praxis and praxis by theory. Added to that,

Christian theologians can confuse the unity of theory and praxis with the unity of faith and action. But in this terminology praxis amounts to both the social determination of our thought-world and active intervention (on the basis of this thought-world) in social relationships, and therefore means far more than doing. Anyone who steadfastly believes in the interpretation which Marxist trends give of our thought-world cannot but suspect that social relationships (viz. praxis) also change ideology (viz. theory). I do not see how Christians can believe that. That the God in whom the Christian church believes is long-suffering, gracious, of great goodness, forgiving evil, to put it in classical terms, and that he raises up the poor from the mire and rewards the meek of the earth is not changed by any praxis, in any sense of the word, as long as we have not yet entered the kingdom of God.

However, to bring this passage to an end, the motive behind the use of this terminology (theory – praxis) is very understandable: theology must be practical, relevant to human life, and not turn into a kind of scholasticism which solves problems that it has raised itself. But we can easily think along those lines in such a way that we only allow the world around us to tell the Christian church what the relevant problems are while the Christian church is not allowed to do the same thing back to the world. Theology does not just have a current market value, dependent on whether it gives a good answer to the problems of the time: it also has an intrinsic value by virtue of its reflections on God and his salvation for human beings and the world. If the throne of God can be established on the hymns of the Christian church, why not on theology, even on speculative theology? Singing hymns is, of course, of little social or political use, but it never has been, and yet the Christian church has gone on doing it down the ages. I see the significance of theology in similar terms. Its credentials may have been questioned, but it does not stand or fall with what the inspectors find in these credentials.

Whether theology – in terms of an academic discipline and an outline proclamation – has a contribution to make to the solution of social problems is a question which the previous comments have not yet resolved. The definitive answer to this question can only be given when we have investigated whether the presence of religious faith can be the foundation for a society or whether it merely reflects this society, or worse, whether it serves as an opium of the people. That

will come later. Here I might just say that theology does not seek
or provide explanations for phenomena of a social or political kind,
for such a theory also calls for a prior analysis, a tool that theology
cannot offer, and so theology *qua* theology cannot provide a basis
for the formation of political power or evaluate directives for
political action. A theologian is not equipped for any of these things.

I deliberately say that a theologian cannot do this *qua* theologian.
But as well as being a theologian, he or she is also a citizen, that is
to say a political and social entity. Here I come up against the other
combination: faith and politics. Whatever faith and politics may
mean in this combination, at all events (and at least) we mean by
the phrase that a citizen in the above-mentioned sense who is at the
same time a Christian does not leave his or her faith behind when
trying to find a way through the jungle of today's political and social
problems. Of course Christians have seldom if ever done that. In
earlier days they may have combined their faith with other political
and social insights, but that does not alter the fact that the anti-
revolutionary Christians of, say, even 1900 were as certain that their
insights were what God wanted as, for example, Christians are
certain about socialism. I shall return to this later in much more
detail, above all to the question how such different insights can be
derived from the same faith. Are they really 'derived from', or is it
a different story?

I shall end with two conclusions: not to leave faith out means
primarily that Christians must not go too quickly past their own
tradition of faith when they are confronted with important political
and social questions, though of course 'not go too quickly past' does
not of itself mean 'derive from'. The other conclusion is that while
anyone who thinks that too much must not be expected of theology
when it comes to social questions is at least leaving theology out of
politics, that is something quite different from leaving out faith or
thinking that faith has nothing to contribute to the good order of a
society.

Yet another combination is the church and politics. The church
is not theology, but it can use theology. Nor is the church the citizen
who does not leave his faith out of things; it is a plurality of
believers who together form a community within a society, a visible
community (it is as impossible to begin with the invisible church as
it is to begin with the invisible state) and therefore a social factor

among other social factors. This basic fact – the church as a social factor – is the starting point for those who argue that the church must not apologize for adopting political standpoints, perhaps using the catchphrase 'You don't *make* yourself a political factor, you already *are* a political factor'. Not to leave faith out of politics now means not to hesitate to introduce statements and actions of the church into the political arena (and thus politics into the church). I shall demonstrate later how limited the possibilities for this are. However, I am approaching things step by step and for the moment want to go no further than to indicate why the combination of church and politics poses problems and what these are connected with. No more than that need be said in this Part.

In the first place the majority of believers who go to make up the church may combine their faith with their political action, but they will not all do so in the same way. To put it in terms of political slogans: there are Christians from the left and right wings, conservatives and progressives, radicals and those who are middle of the road, feminists, and supporters of the family and so on. And all the time the church is an institution, and institutions presuppose that people do at least some things right, since that is what makes an institution an institution. So the first problem we come up against is an internal problem. As an institution the church presupposes united action, but in reality this unity does not exist. That means that either the church is not an institution from the perspective of political action, or political action is not a function of the church as an institution, or at any rate does not make it an institution. In both cases the question is, how can the church then speak or act politically *qua* church?

The reason why this problem is so easily passed over is connected with the twofold way in which the word church is used, often in the same sentence: as a description and a norm. Used descriptively the word denotes the church as it actually is in its function as a social factor (and thus without any unity of political action) and in a normative sense it also denotes the church as it should be or as it may be seen in faith. Both approaches have their justification, but something goes wrong if we do not keep them separate. We can then hear someone talking about what he or she thinks that the church is and does – cares for the poor or is the conscience of politics – whereas in fact the church is not that at all and the speaker also knows that very well, since that is precisely what he or she is saying. The 'is' means 'must be' or 'needs to be'. When people talk about the church speaking and acting politically, we do not know which sense they are using. They are talking about the church as a social factor, since it must speak and act politically. At the same time they are talking about the paper church, the church in books, since as a social factor it does not speak politically but is divided at precisely this point. What in fact happens is that, however powerful it may sound, the speaker is appropriating the word church for what he or she personally – and not a large number of fellow Christians – thinks that the church must be, say and do. That would not be so bad if that were all that were said, but what is actually said is that the church as a social factor supports social standpont X and political standpoint Y, while all the time we can see clearly that as a social factor the church harbours five or six standpoints within it. The result is then confusion and offence, achieved with the help of the ambiguous use of the word church.

This brings me to the second problem in which the combination of church and politics lands us: no matter how the church may try to wriggle out of the fact, as an institution it is at the same time a power factor. It may play that role reluctantly, or it can enjoy it; it can make use of it or repudiate it, but that is what it is, at least in the situation with which we are familiar. But does the church – in the way in which Christians themselves interpret it – act in so simple a way in exercising political power? The church stands for the other world of God, the opposite kind of world where things are done not through power or violence but through the Spirit of God. If that is its status, how can a church act at a political level without contradicting itself? We shall have to return to this problem in detail in the part of the book which deals with the way in which the church may make political and social statements. However, at that point we shall have to sort out a prior problem: who or what in fact speaks as the church?

For the moment, to end with, I would point out that theology is not the same thing as faith and these two things are not the same as the church, although all three concepts are connected. Therefore the way in which the three terms can be connected with politics is also different in each case. So we must look carefully to see what can and what cannot be expected of faith, church and theology on a political level. That is what this book is about.

But how does it happen that all three combinations – faith and politics, theology and politics and church and politics – are so often used interchangeably, so that they seem to be about the same thing? In the first place the believer who sets himself up as a political and social activist with the backing of his faith is (or usually is) at the same time a member of the church and in some cases also a theologian. The same person may be acting all the time, but he or she is acting at different times in different capacities. We can see that most clearly if we take as an example a theologian whom we hear expressing a political standpoint. Are we then listening to a theologian who is putting the result of his or her theological investigation on the table or to a citizen with political concerns who is at the same time a Christian and has adopted a particular standpoint in the light of being a Christian? I would go for the latter alternative, arguing that the expression of the standpoint is not a theological statement but a political statement, in this case by a Christian. The fact that the speaker is a theologian does not alter things in the slightest. Not everything that a theologian says is theology, nor does something become theology through being said by a theologian (any more than something becomes sociology through being said by a sociologist). Anyone who fails to keep this simple truth in mind will already think that the statements of theologians are theological statements and this will give rise to or confirm the mistaken view that Christians get political directives from theology.

Can theologians themselves not avoid such misunderstandings by saying, 'I am now speaking as someone socially and politically active who is at the same time a Christian'? Certainly, but a number of theologians do not want to do that, because they do in fact think that Christians can and must go to theology in order to get guidelines for their politics. Here I come to the second cause of the overlapping of the terms church, faith and theology, but instead of talking about causes I must now talk in terms of reasons because there is now a theological motive for this overlapping. Because the matter is so important I shall devote a separate chapter, the next one, to this theological motive.

4. *Theology is not criticism of society*

It may be a matter of loose terminology that church, faith and theology seem to mean the same thing, but it may be that a particular view of theology lies behind it. In that case we must not talk in terms of confusion but of a theological motive. This is the direction taken by Karl Barth and his successors. We shall often come across the name of Barth, not so much because of all kinds of doctrinal innovations that he introduced – though that is also the case – but because of his answer to the question how we know at all. Barth gives a different answer to that from the answer given by classical theology, an answer with such far-reaching consequences that we can indeed see it as representing all kinds of doctrinal innovation. What form does the answer take?

To sum him up briefly, Barth says that it is not only useless but even reprehensible to see knowledge of God as the end-point of a way of knowledge. To speak about God makes sense only if we begin from the reality that God has revealed himself in Jesus Christ: any other start is a false start and leads nowhere, is at most a sign that we do not accept God as he really is. Anyone who does not begin with God never gets to God. Barth works out this basic philosophy very powerfully and very consistently in his theological outline. Since we must begin with the reality that God has revealed himself in Jesus Christ, the Christian church does not and need not know anything but him. Jesus Christ is the one Word of God that the church proclaims. Theology is a service to proclamation, by putting it into words; not, however, expressing something that comes from outside but – and this is quite consistent – something that comes from within, from the Word of God itself, by which the church lives. Moreover, for Barth theology is an internal concern of the church: it is a form of proclamation, albeit at a higher level.

These comments bring us to the heart of the theme of this chapter, since this means that the church (which proclaims), the proclamation of faith, and theology (as a higher form of proclamation) can be interchangeable concepts: at all events, concepts which in fact can be used interchangeably with impunity, as is evident for example from the work of Gollwitzer and Jüngel, who are both followers of Barth's basic philosophy. For there is always only one Word of God, Jesus Christ, and if this is all that the church knows and proclaims, and theology helps here, it does not matter whether you talk in terms of church and politics, faith and politics or theology and politics: you are always concerned with the same thing, namely with the one Word of God and therefore proclamation, the church which proclaims, and theology, when you want to know what to do as a Christian, even in politics.

I shall return many times in this book to the theme of the one Word of God; each time from a different perspective, because it plays a important role in the development that I am describing here, a negative one, as we shall see. At this stage I can add two comments. The first I can keep short because I have said more about it in another context. I do not agree with Barth's answer to the question 'How do you know that?'. To say that anyone who does not begin with God, with the reality that God has revealed himself in Jesus Christ, never gets to God, is an exaggeration, and the way in which Barth develops it in his doctrine of the one Word of God is even more exaggerated. When we are thinking of the presupposition of all our knowledge of God, Barth's argument is not only plausible but indispensable: how could we know God if God's reality were not the foundation of our knowledge? But in that case we are concerned with the being of things and the order which applies there. Knowing does not follow the order of being but has its own order, a sequential order. Let me illustrate this from the Christian doctrine of creation. According to this doctrine all human beings are creatures of God – to use a characteristic expression of Barth's – whether they know it or not. This last phrase is what I mean. In the order of being all human beings are God's creatures, but it does not follow from this that they know that they are. If that knowledge is to come into being, it has to follow a way of its own: someone must communicate it, it must meet up with the experience of others, this experience must then be shown to be an authentic one, and so on. Barth neglects the order of knowing and deals too lightly with the question how we know for certain that God has revealed himself

– exclusively – in Jesus Christ by saying that there is only one answer to this: it is so. Classical theology left room for questioning, for arguments and even for testing insights and experience, since for classical theology God was not unknown to human beings as the result of a form of general revelation. Believers and non-believers had a particular sphere in common, so conversation between them was possible. Barth will have none of this. The Word of God begins with itself, so the church begins with itself and so does proclamation and therefore also theology.

This brings me to my second comment. I do not share the concept of theology which is connected with Barth's outline; on the contrary, I think it extremely unfortunate both because of its theological presuppositions and because of its practical consequences. I have already gone into the theological presuppositions, and in due course I shall return to them and clarify and extend my criticism. Here I shall concentrate on the practical consequences, since that follows naturally from the previous chapter. On the basis of the construction of the exclusive, one Word of God which contains all that we must know and which is proclaimed through the church, theology is in principle saddled with all human questions, including questions relating to social and political action. In this way – on theological grounds – it is forced into a role which it cannot fulfil, however broadly it may be defined. Theology cannot give an answer to all the questions with which both Christians and non-Christians are faced. The theological faculty offers the preacher a training cobbled on the academic last and that profession cannot be better defined than in the classical terms of being pastor and teacher to the Christian community. The students or theologians who have been produced by this faculty therefore have not acquired any skills in social and political questions: they have not been trained for trade union work or for organizing activities. Of course these too are important functions and occupations, perhaps even more important than those of a preacher. But the theological faculty does not provide any insight into all these areas: it does not have the conceptual apparatus through which such insight must be gained, nor criteria with the help of which it can be tested. Therefore it cannot give any answer to the specific questions which arise in these spheres. Anyone who begins to study theology in order to help people has good intentions, but he or she must remember that people can be helped in many ways, that there are many ways of being trained to give help and that theology is only of use in giving help which is called for through the human need for belief in God and can also be given there. Anyone who does not see that, or hardly sees it, and still wants to help people to get through life must not go to a theological faculty but somewhere else.

However, there is another consequence of this. The Christian church can use the fruits of theological study, but it needs more than theology if it is to know the ropes and continue to do so in the sometimes chaotic reality of social and political developments.

But does God have anything to do with this? If theology wants to help people to follow the traces of God, then does theology have to do with everything? It is true that theology is about God and that anyone who talks about God is talking about everything, or God would not be God. Moreover, as far as that is concerned, it is neither strange nor perverse that theology should also talk about politics and society. Anyone who recalls how readily theologians from earlier generations occupied themselves with scientific theories about, for example, the origin of the stellar systems need not be surprised that theologians today are ready to pass judgment on all kinds of social theories.

At the same time I should indicate the limitations of this kind of exercise. The theologians from the last century whom I mentioned did not really know about the stellar world but derived their knowledge from others. The same is true of theologians today: they themselves have not studied society. At best they are trained in social philosophy and ethics and have read their newspapers as citizens. They can therefore join in discussions depending on the degree of wisdom and knowledge of things that they have acquired in these areas. But they are not occupied here with their professional work. Although God has to do with everything and in this sense so has theology, theology does not know everything and not everything is theology (and of course theology is not everything).

The sense in which theology has to do with everything is defined by the perspective from which it approaches reality: it looks at human beings and the world in so far as people claim to have experience there of God, his promises of salvation and his command; it tests what people say and so helps both the church and the world to speak in terms of salvation and commandments about God's ways

with human beings and the world. Thus in fact theology is concerned
with everything, but it is concerned with everything in so far as
God's promises of salvation and commandments are concerned with
everything.

The more specific the terms are which theology uses in this
connection, in other words, the more it moves in areas where other
professional disciplines provide knowledge, the more vulnerable
and time-conditioned it appears, and the more it has to be on its
guard not to do again something that others have already done
earlier and better. We already know what democracy is (through,
say, Rousseau, Tom Paine and Montesquieu); we already know
that torturing prisoners, exploiting the weak and murdering the
innocent is wrong: there are fixed rules which are known in every
society. We do not need theology to discover all that. Of course
theology too can talk about it, the Christian tradition knows that.
And Christian proclamation can make a point of it, indeed must do
so if people forget. But we know all that without bringing theology
into it. If theologians use their profession to say what we already
know or what others know, then they do superfluous work, duplicate. By duplication I mean doing yet again with theological arguments – often bad ones, since the discipline does not lend itself to
this sort of thing – what others already did before them (and usually
better). Through duplication theology makes itself superfluous. If
that is all there is to be said, others soon take over its work.

After duplication, especially where political and social questions
are raised by theologians, we come to simplification. Let me give
one example which in my view is convincing enough: the use of the
word politics.

In one of the previous chapters we noted that the term politics
has two components and that for this reason it sparks off passions:
1. political ideals and 2. the gaining of power to realize these ideals.
It is an utter simplification of politics if the second element, the
struggle for power, is left out. Yet that happens with many theologians who talk about politics. When Karl Barth says that faith is
always 'utterly political', he means that not just the individual but
also society is the concern of Christian faith. Or if Pannenberg says
that the kingdom of God is a political concept he wants to stress that
God's promises concern individuals *and* society. The same is true
of Moltmann's statement that Jesus' action was always pre-eminently

political. But these are definitions of politics which do not cost anyone – either church or believer – anything: the element of the power struggle has been left out and this is precisely the component which, even more than the political ideal, makes the combinations of faith and politics, church and politics and theology and politics so precarious.

Duplication proves superfluous, simplification does not help. What then? That is certainly not so easy, above all when we remember that theology does not just consist in scientific testing but also includes an outline proclamation. It is certainly clear how vulnerable a theologian is, above all when his other outline proclamation enters the sphere of politics and the social sciences. The rest of the book will make that repeatedly clear.

I am not arguing that theologians must keep away from this area, though perhaps that might be a conclusion arrived at in the course of this book. But if they do involve themselves in it they would do better to keep to their own skills and begin with what people say about God, especially when they do so in terms of politics and social theories and directives. Theology does not have to invent these theories; nor did it invent the theory of evolution. But that is no reason not to go into the question whether 'the name of the Lord' is used vainly in them – or, the opposite possibility – wrongly left out. In doing this, theology remains in its own sphere: and then it can be strong and critical.

I see that I have spoken about theology and theological arguments and not about sociological explanations of theological statements or about standpoints of faith. Theology tests what human beings say about God and does not explain in political or social terms why they say it. To try to give sociological explanations – if they may be called that – is a legitimate concern but it is not theology; theologians are not trained to do this, and so here too they can only echo the remarks of others. They may indeed do that, just as they may make use of social theories or political ideals, but it remains a precarious undertaking. I shall return to it.

It seems to me that within the framework of the questions raised in this Part, with the difficulties from both theological theory and practice, I have produced enough arguments against Barth's view of theology and that of his pupils: it gives rise to the confusion of terms against which I am writing here. Let us keep to the facts, 1.

that theology is a limited scientific discipline, certainly if we see the discipline in terms of professional training; 2. that believers need not be theologians to be able to think and act as Christians, any more than a person needs to be a sociologist to be able to engage in social work; and 3. that the church and believers need more than theology if they are to play a responsible role – each according to his or her capacities – in the sphere of political and social power.

Here I have completed a first demarcation which in some respects has been a first reconnaissance. Let me sum up my standpoint. As far as faith and politics are concerned, if we mean by that that a Christian becomes involved in gaining political power to realize political ideals *because* he or she is a Christian, that is my standpoint. That is not to make any decision on the question of what ideals can be reconciled with being a Christian and what methods can be used. I shall discuss that later. It is enough for me here to say that if a Christian – to use the language of our grandfathers – understands his or her Christian duty, he or she will be wholeheartedly involved in politics (both components). But I would not go on to say, for example, that one must be a Christian to know what good politics is; on the contrary, I shall repeat many times that both in politics and in the field of social morality the norms by which action needs to be tested do not come from the Bible or Christian faith nor need they derive from that to be decisive in guiding Christians over what is good and what is bad or, if you like, Christian and non-Christian politics. They were already there before the Bible; they were good and therefore we also find them in the Bible.

'Church and politics' is a combination over which I am much more hesitant. For many reasons I cannot see the church taking part in the political power struggle without losing its nature as church. The relationship with politics (both elements) is unavoidable and even necessary, but it is more difficult and more precarious than the relationship which the Christian *qua* citizen has to politics and certainly does not primarily become established through theology. Here I have also already indicated my conclusions about theology and politics: whatever else theology may be, it is not criticism of society (it has no criteria for that) nor theory for action, in terms of a normative theory for political action or a programme for it. It cannot be all those things without ceasing to be theology: scientific testing of what people know about God on the one hand and an outline proclamation of God and his salvation on the other.

Here we have not yet exhausted what is to be said about theology. It could be that what I have just written has been written by someone who does not understand himself, far less know himself as a theologian. In that case he must go to the social or political psychiatrist, who can see what he himself cannot see, trapped as he is in his class consciousness or, less seriously, in his social determination. In the following Part we shall go to visit the psychiatrist. Perhaps he is trapped himself.

Bibliography

K.Barth, *Church Dogmatics* I-IV, T.&.T.Clark 1936ff.

J.Berting et al., *Elites komen, elites gaan*, Baarn 1976

H.Gollwitzer, *Forderungen der Umkehr*, Munich 1976

S.Hampshire (ed.), *Public and Private Morality*, Cambridge University Press 1978

H.M.Kuitert, 'Het vrije veld van de theologie', in *In rapport met de tijd. 100 jaar theologie aan de Vrije Universiteit*, Kampen 1980, 236-51

G.Manenschijn, *Eigenbelang en christelijke ethiek*, Baarn 1982

G.H.Sabine and T.L.Thorson, *A History of Political Theory*, Hinsdale, Ill., ⁴1973

M.Walzer, 'Political Action: The Problem of Dirty Hands', in M.Cohen, T.Nagel and T.Scanlon, *War and Moral Responsibility*, Princeton University Press 1974, 62-82

The list of titles at the end of each Part does not cover the works on which the Part is based (I have read more than is listed there), far less the most important books on the theme discussed (there are many more important ones) but a selection of the enormous amount of literature on the subject, a selection which is not arbitrary in that it indicates works which will quickly give the reader an insight into the problem discussed in the Part.

II Religion and Society

5. Religious faith and the social sciences

We would make it too easy for ourselves if after a first survey we went on to apply a theological perspective to the relationship between religious faith and politics. That would be to pass over an important intermediary stage: is religious faith, are church and theology, clear about themselves? Believers are confident in their conviction that reality corresponds to their faith and that religion therefore has a contribution of its own to make which, as far as politics is concerned, cannot be reduced to something else. But a considerable number of people think otherwise, not just because they do not believe what believers believe but, taking it a stage further, because they offer an explanation for the existence or even the survival of religious faith which at the same time explains away this faith. Religious faith does not have a contribution of its own to make but is a contingent epiphenomenon of human forms of society and derives from that according to some its value and according to others its uselessness.

Here we come up against the modern criticism of religion which especially since the nineteenth century has become enormously popular but which – I should add – has also made things particularly easy for itself and still does. The gist of the criticism can be quickly stated: religion (I shall also use religion instead of faith or religious faith in this Part) serves to consolidate systems. The whole of society looks for change, emancipation and freedom, and religion holds up the development.

Religion of course includes the Christian religion in particular and thus the Christianity institutionalized in the churches, in which the Christian religion now exists among us. What it amounts to is that people who want to change society come up against the tenacious immaturity of faith. As can be seen, that is the religious criticism of – to make it easy – the left. Does that judgment correspond with Christian religious faith? The vigour with which some Christians are active as Christians and at the same time as members of the left wing might make one think that they in fact subscribe to this view, but in fact they want to show that things can be different: Christian faith can also be a power for change.

What I now want to assert – and it is the essence of this Part – is that we cannot even say yes or no to this question ('is the criticism correct?'), nor should we begin to do so, since the way the question is put is wrong. If we put it like that we have already accepted the relevance of religious faith for a particular political development – of the left or right, to say it again – as a criterion for judging whether religion passes the test, and acceptance of the criterion in turn goes back to – or at least comes much too close to being – an explanation of religious faith in terms of its significance for society (for better or worse).

Later I shall bring out in detail what explanation means here. For the moment I would point out that it is not only typically Marxist to explain the existence (and continuance) of religion in this way but that it is also bourgeois – as the term is used of anti-Marxist philosophers and sociologists – to be preoccupied with this kind of explanation. We shall also see that in due course.

For the moment the important thing is for Christians not to allow themselves to be persuaded that the significance of their faith stands or falls with its social or political relevance. Certainly Christian faith is also of social or political importance, and if it is not so then we must see that it is. However, I repeat yet again that anyone who allows its worth, importance or relevance to be defined by the degree to which it is involved with right-wing or left-wing political strategies – it can be claimed by both – has *a priori* given away the criterion for good or bad religion and made God, faith, church and theology authorities which are at the service of politics. And that is something that church and theology do not set out to be and have never set out to be. But they need not think along these lines, because of either the justifiable need to consider intellectual honesty or the equally justifiable feeling that Christians must remain faithful to the earth, since the conclusion that religious faith is a function of society (or a society) is premature. Not only must Christian faith oppose such an interpretation – more about that later – the theories of the social sciences about religion and society can make such a standpoint impossible. This Part will above all be about that. Here I shall analyse as far as possible what has been said about the connection between religion and society, in other words between religion and forms of society, and this analysis would seem to be the best defence against the tug of sociological explanations of religious faith.

Of course I cannot give a complete list of the claims of sociologists of religion here, nor is that necessary for my purposes. I am not contemplating any sociological criticism of sociologists, but will only take into account any theological interest in their theories. Nor am I interested in the finer points of the matter – here at any rate – since I am concerned with the broad outline of their portrayal of the mutual relationships between religion and society.

Ultimately I want to find an answer to two questions (and theories from the sociology of religion must help me to find them): 1. Is religion necessary for the continued existence of a society? 2. Is religion a factor which furthers processes of change in a society or not? Both questions have an empirical slant: a society *seems* to need religion and religion *seems* to be a force for change, or the opposite, or something else. In this way I shall remain on the level of the social sciences with their empirical approach. So I am not asking – here at any rate – whether religion is indispensable or *should* be a factor for change. The first question is connected with, among other things, the whole complex of questions which are usually summed up under the heading of secularization; in other words, a society can do without religion. Or is that going too far and does secularization simply mean that society can do without an authoritative church? We shall see. The answer to the second question is important because, to put it crudely, it could indicate whether religion forces people to the right or to the left. When I say religion I am thinking of Christian religion, given that religion does not exist without people who unite around a number of tenets of faith, so I am thinking of groups, churches and tendencies in which this faith is more or less institutionalized.

There is another term which needs to be clarified: I have just spoken about religion and society and not about faith and politics. That does not imply a change of subject but there are reasons for the change in terminology. One of them is trivial: this is how sociologists talk and in these chapters I am taking over their terminology. But there is another advantage in the change: we have already come across the term society a number of times and will continue to do so. Now we have the opportunity to define it and at the same time to relate it to what has been summarized under the heading of politics. Society is a co-ordinating concept. Sociologists understand by it an organized, durable entity which reproduces itself as a group in which social organization on the one hand (the social and political order) and culture on the other (norms, values, faith) have a reciprocal relationship. So politics and faith – if we focus more closely on our theme – presuppose each other. But how, and do they still do that, or is this time past?

First it will have become quite clear why we consult immediately a descriptive (and interpretative) discipline like sociology and do not also – in the light of Christian faith itself – try to establish what should be the connection between society and religious faith. We would get nowhere with our normative ideas about this if we did not first establish what problems can be solved in that field and what are the alternatives between which a choice must be made.

A second reason why I shall be first discussing the sociologists and then specifically the results of their investigations into religion and society is that in that way we shall first as it were allow outsiders to have a word and not just work with the views of outsiders. The risk for all those who speak from within is that they may not be sufficiently aware of themselves, if they take faith, theology and the church into the sphere of politics. That was the excuse with which I began this chapter.

A third reason is almost self-evident: theology can make statements about God and society; one of the next Parts will be doing that. Sociologists cannot. But theology cannot make an empirical investigation of religion and society: it does not have the tools, let alone the experience which is needed. If we want to know something about society as it is we must go to the social scientists whether we want to or not. And why should we not want to, if they can protect us from our naivety and folly? Religion is always religion *in* and sometimes *of* a particular society. That is one of the reasons why the same religious faith, including Christian faith, can vary from culture to culture. In terms of the useful illustration provided by Abraham Kuyper: the yeast may well be the same but the kind of bread that is made from it depends on the dough. Religious faith does something with a society – to take that as a starting point – but a society also does something with religious faith. Those who will not accept what sociological investigation tells us about that will go astray. They will fail to see how easily faith is, or becomes, the ideological opposite to the ideal of a particular society (in political terms, right-wing or left-wing), far less be on their guard against this. They will tend to overestimate (or perhaps underestimate) by putting the role of faith too high (or too low) and not in the middle: they will make vague generalizations about things which cannot be quantified, for example whether religious faith is really disappearing from society as some theologians of secularization have been arguing for years or whether these theologians want it to decline so that all that is left is what may be called faith according to their own definition.

A last question is whether religious faith is accessible to so empirically orientated an investigation as that of sociology. By and large we can distinguish three answers to this question. The first is that religious faith – if it is taken seriously – of individuals and groups is not dependent on social factors but on God himself in his revelation. So it is not determined by social factors and thus falls outside the scope of so empirical a discipline as sociology. This standpoint has been adopted by some theologians. From a socio-logical perspective it means that religion is seen as an autonomous, self-regulating segment of human reality, which can clearly be differentiated from segments like politics and economics and thus also cannot be corrupted by what happens there.

A variant of this view – which can be based on other presuppo-sitions – is that the sociology of religion can investigate other religions or church communities than those to which the investigator belongs but never the one of which he or she is a part.

The opposite answer begins from the presupposition that there is no mystery at all in religious faith which would be a reason why it should escape scientific investigation. It is a social phenomenon which is an epiphenomenon of other, 'harder' phenomena, for example in the social order, and must therefore be treated accord-ingly. Along these lines it is argued that sociology is the scientific explanation of religion, explaining here being tantamount to deriving it from non-religious factors and thus explaining it away. This process can easily be seen; we find it wherever the formula is used, 'X is none other than Y'. The Marxist criticism of religion –

understood as sociology – is a prime example of such an explanation (explaining away) of religion.

The two answers which I have mentioned so far price themselves out of the market by their one-sidedness. There is a third standpoint on the matter, and that seems to me well capable of defence. God may well be and remain the final mystery of religious faith, but it is not for the sociologist in his or her professional capacity to talk about him, even if he or she is a believer. Nor does the discipline of sociology call for that, since this discipline investigates empirical activities, organizations and concerns in so far as these fulfil a function in a society. Religious faith also has an empirical side and plays a role which can be noted empirically, and sociology can describe and interpret this. However, sociologists must remember – as they do if they keep to their brief – that religion need not be exhausted by its social activities or forms of organization. Therefore sociologists may very well be investigators and committed believers at the same time.

There is one limit beyond which neither sociologists nor theologians can go: in each case their investigation and interpretation takes place within a given socio-cultural system which presupposes its own pattern of values and norms that the investigator cannot escape. An absence of cultural bias – to put it in broad terms – does not exist: no one can transcend our historical limits. What one can do is to be aware of these limits and try to make good use of them, for example in avoiding partisanship in an investigation once it has begun and in publishing the results – even in the sociology of religion – as something worth looking at.

To sum up: the investigation in which we shall now steep ourselves is concerned with the reciprocal influences exerted by religious faith and society as a social and cultural system in which this faith is an element. It is quite certain that society also does something to religion. But what, and to what conclusion should that lead us?

6. Religion serves to consolidate systems: the functionalist and Marxist interpretation

For people who would very much like to see religious faith being used for social and political revolutions, it is a disappointing experience to find that religious faith is opposed to this usage. But that is the only conclusion that can be drawn from practice. Churches – the most institutionalized form of Christian religion – are overwhelmingly conservative. In this respect there is an enormous gulf between the theoretical conceptions of Christian faith with which theologians work and what church people actually believe. Progressive Christians have experienced that all their lives: there is no tougher problem than the church. Not only practice but investigation and theory confirm this position. We shall be discussing all three in these chapters. I shall try to make it clear – with the help of what sociologists of religion have said – that religious faith, including Christian faith, does not just have a conservative effect but is also by nature conservative when it comes to relations with society, so that it is understandable that one side (Marx) despises this religion and the other side (bourgeois sociologists) praises it. Thus bourgeois and Marxist sociology share the view that religious faith serves to consolidate a system but differ when it comes to the question whether the social system should be consolidated. I shall come back to this strange situation shortly. What I am now going to do is to demonstrate the unanimity of the sociologists – for all their differences – over the role or the significance (both words are used here to express the 'contribution to') of religious faith for society. I use society in the singular because for convenience I shall keep to the society that we know best, namely the Western society to which we belong.

There can be no question here of my discussing all the theories about the sociology of religion. I have no room for that, and moreover anyone with that intention would have to be a sociologist. Here I am simply keeping in view my two questions: 1. Does society depend on religion? 2. Can religion be called a factor for change? Or, to put them together, does religious faith make a contribution to society, and if so, of what kind?

Mady Thung's tripartite division provides a convenient way of organizing the material: religion as the factor that integrates society (in that case we are following in the steps of Durkheim); religion as a compensating factor for a society which has gone wrong (Marx and his followers); and religion as a factor in the secularization of Western capitalist society (Weber and the theologians of secularization). This provides a division into three instead of a division into two (bourgeois-Marxist). That need not be confusing, since I include Durkheim and Weber among the bourgeois, non-Marxist sociologists, though of course they differ over method (Weber's approach is more phenomenological and that of Durkheim more positivistic, though neither of them falls completely into these categories) but not in presuppositions: religion serves to consolidate society, and if religion disappears, who or what must then take over its role?

So it does not matter very much whether the division is into two or three, in so far as this presupposition is shared by all three approaches. As a result all three present themselves as variants of what is called a functional approach to religious faith (in Marx and Weber, Christian faith in so many words). Such an approach is plausible. For the social sciences religious faith, embodied in an institution made up of its adherents, is a social phenomenon amidst other social phenomena and what sociologists investigate, among other things, is the functional relationship (who does what with whom) between the different phenomena among themselves and between the phenomena and the whole of society. Such a functional approach raises problems. We shall encounter them in due course and use them in a criticism of this approach. But it is worth the trouble nevertheless to classify the theories. Apart from that the social sciences would prove an uninteresting conversation partner and we would deprive ourselves of insight into the relationship between religion and society. We can also learn a good deal from theories about which we are critical.

(a) *Religious faith as an intergrating factor* (Durkheim). Although he was an atheist, Durkheim was fascinated by the phenomenon of religion. He found that evolutionists like Tylor and Frazer were wrong: religion is not a fossil in the making; on the contrary, it is the power which holds a society together and therefore an indispensible structural element for the whole (and one of the most interesting phenomena for sociology). The Australian totem religions were his evidence: these religions show that religion consists in worshipping the holy, divine, totem animal, but what in fact is worshipped in the totem is one's own society. The totem (for example a crow) integrates the members of the clan (who see one another as crows), informs them (shows them that as well as crows there are also kangaroos and eagles) and gives them directives for action (impresses on them what crows do in contrast to others). He applied this approach to modern European societies: there too he thought that we must imagine society as being held together by religion and as with the Australian religions we must then think of religion not as worship of an abstract God but as the worship of society – or better, common life – itself, as a result of which social cohesion and moral consensus, the necessary conditions for any society, are given the surplus value which explains and guarantees their existence. The question at this point is whether 1. Durkheim means that religious figures (God, totem) are simply symbolic terms for the society itself and is therefore occupied in explaining religion by explaining it away or 2. whether he means almost the opposite – that we cannot speak of society other than in terms of God and the holy. If the latter is the case, then his theory is not concerned to explain away religion but presupposes 'God' and 'the holy', using them to explain how it can be that social cohesion and moral consensus can be achieved. In that case in its religion society worships not so much itself as it is as the wonder of living together, God as the source of social cohesion and moral consensus.

This latter interpretation – and there is much to support it – makes Durkheim something other than the down-to-earth positivist that he is made out to be in many popular discussions. The theme that he touches on here – religion as the necessary condition for the ongoing existence of society – was to preoccupy sociologists of religion from then on, and his functional account – religion socializes through internalizing – remains relevant to the present day.

(*b*) *Religion as a compensating factor* (Marx). The occasion for Marx's criticism of religion was the struggle against a ruling class opposed to social change. Marx sees the church and religious faith as the means by which this class tries to maintain its position. However, there is no need to exterminate the church and religion, since they will disappear of their own accord. For religion is a form of thinking that has gone wrong (or reflection on the wrong things) in a society which has gone wrong. Had society been well ordered, there would have been no religion, for the simple reason that no one would have needed it, just as – to follow Engels – a good society would have no need of 'You shall not steal', since there would be no private property.

To make his position acceptable, Marx developed his scheme of foundation and superstructure, with his starting point in the worker as the authentic human being. First of all it is asserted that the determinative forces in or of a society are economic and social: productive forces (viz. human work in the natural world with the help of technology), productive relationships (viz. private property, especially in connection with the means of production). What the superstructure looks like (viz. what people regard as valuable) is determined by the infrastructure (viz. how productive forces and relationships develop from one another, for example in the form of a class struggle). That is what Marx calls his materialism: it is meant as an explanatory principle. What is the state of the infrastructure in Europe? It has gone wrong. The few – the owners of the means of production – enjoy the fruits of the labours of very many. They form the ruling class and defend their position which has grown up through history by means of their ideology (viz. the thought-world determined by their interests). For Marx religion, especially the Christian religion, was ideology par excellence. It disguises the real state of affairs, weakens the chances of protest, leads a pseudo-life (it has no substructure other than that people in fact suffer and therefore reach for the opium of religion) and is sold by the ruling class as 'damaged goods' to the workers to keep them subjected and docile. Thus Marx detested the Christian religion above all because of the social quietism that he found in it. Christianity and protest against the existing order are mutually exclusive.

It emerges from this that Marx too begins from the view that the function of religious faith is to hold society together. However, his materialism makes him believe that you must attack these tangles of injustice not at the superstructure, the ideology, but at the infrastructure. The rest – including religious faith – will then fall of its own accord. A modern tendency in Marxism is no longer so sure about that. The dispute at the ideological level must be carried out at the same time, they say, because the supporting role of the ideology (whether consolidating the system or revolutionary) is stronger and more significant than people have long assumed. A number of Christians see this development – the attribution of a relative autonomy to religion and morality – as an opportunity to combine Christianity and Marxism. And in fact in this way of thinking religious faith has a much greater chance in society – including a much greater chance of survival – than in orthodox Marxism. Church and Christianity can also stand on the right side of the dividing line as 'ideological apparatus' (Althusser).

However, we can hardly mistake the fact that this Marxist trend speaks of *relative* autonomy – it would cease to be Marxist if it did otherwise. In the last instance productive forces and relationships are the decisive function: the substructure and not the superstructure. There is a further question: if Christian faith has only a functional relationship to society, may it serve only as an ideological argument? I shall come back to that in the next chapter.

(*c*) *Religion as a secularizing factor* (Weber). For Weber, as for Durkheim, the intertwining of religion and society is a central datum. What connects him with Marx is the historical question, what contribution has Christian religion made to the development of our Western society? Or, to put it rather more precisely, what are the conditions for the origin of our highly developed Western culture? Weber replies that this culture is not the product of a natural development but of rationality, i.e. of people acting rationally. Where does the rationality come from and why did it develop specifically in the West? This is where Weber introduces the Christian religion. This religion has taught us that God is 'beyond', transcendent, and does not coincide with nature or the world. In other words, Christian faith makes the world around us open to a rational approach. Martin Buber later repeated this position, as did A.T.van Leeuwen after that.

But what does history show us? Religious faith and rationality go their own ways; the effect of religion on the development of society

is different from what one might think and can only be defined by
an accurate historical study. Weber himself made such a study in
The Protestant Ethic and the Spirit of Capitalism (1904). I shall not
discuss this study but only bring out what Weber wanted to show by
it.

First of all he wanted to demonstrate that ideas, for example
religious ideas, are independent factors in historical processes: they
can make a formative contribution. That is an anti-Marxist position.
On the other hand ideas, however spiritual or lofty they may be,
always function in existing spheres of interest of many kinds and
that also means that their real effects (e.g. social effects) can seem
very different from what their adherents themselves intend. Ideas,
too, determine history, are conditions for the origin of developments, cannot be left out of an explanation of them but cannot
explain everything; the material context within which they are set
also determines their final effect. This last point is also against the
Marxists.

Weber's second concern was to show that Western rationalism
has gone its own way. Having begun as an element in a process of
religious development, it now exists without religion: in other words,
it does not need religion to explain it. That is Weber's interpretation
of so-called secularization: religionless rationality is an effect of
religion itself.

That ends the survey of the three approaches in the sociology of
religion to which I shall attach my comments. In all three, religion
is approached in a functional way. So I shall first sum up the basic
presuppositions from which the functionalists among the sociologists
of religion begin and by which they can be recognized. First of all,
they argue from the whole of an existing social and cultural system,
and secondly, they ask what effect a partial system, for example
religious faith, has on the existence of the whole.

A first comment that I would make here is that in this approach
the status or desirability of the whole (from which the argument
begins) is not subjected to a test. People certainly pass judgment on
it, whether negatively (Marx) or positively (the bourgeois sociologists), but that judgment does not lie in or follow from the
functionalist theory. It indicates only the way in which religion
functions towards the whole. It has a stabilizing effect or consolidates
the system because it takes in the individual and prevents him or

her from being a disruptive factor towards the whole through anonymous behaviour (as it is called in Durkheim), an honest disposition (Marx) or disorientation (Parsons). The question whether religious faith is functional in respect of the individual or of society is therefore solved here by arguing that precisely through having significance for the individual it contributes to the stability of the whole, indeed that it makes an indispensable contribution towards it. Religion, like politics, law, language and so on, is a structural and functional requirement of or for a society (Parsons).

However, that brings us up against a new complex of questions. Does such a functionalist view fit with the actual situation which suggests to us – not entirely without reason – that religion is on the way back? Does a society – certainly Western society – then have to disintegrate? But that is not happening. In that case what does hold a society together? Or is it rather premature to say that religion is in process of vanishing? Luckmann solves this problem by saying that while religion in the churches is declining, on the basis of the social cohesion and moral consensus which still exist – here we hear Durkheim speaking – we must suppose that religion is present, but that it is an invisible religion, a collective universe of meaning or significance, into which individuals are born. Socialization is and remains internalization.

According to others that is too good to be true. So-called secularization is not about the loss of function in the churches but about religious faith as such. Religion is no longer an integrating factor. The best indication of this is the pluralism of world views. There is no longer any religion which is shared by the whole of society. That is the standpoint of Peter Berger, followed e.g. by Mady Thung. It seems to me difficult to settle this difference of opinion in an empirical way. Such a symbolic universe can be demonstrated without many problems when it is a matter of more or less closed groups within society, but in that case there is more than one universe. However, we must extend or dilute the concept of religion considerably if we want to be able to demonstrate such a universe, say in Dutch society as a whole. In that case we would end up with a form of civil religion (in the sense in which Bellah talks about it), but even then it is one thing to be happy with such a religion – it would spare us situations like that in Lebanon – and something else to show that it really exists. We should also be able to combine both positions: there is a plurality of cognitive minorities (as Berger calls the members of a symbolic universe) in our society and at the same time they all share a belief in the indispensable value of plurality, for example in the way in which Kolakowski describes the support for this value as a faith characteristic of Europe.

As I have said, I need not solve this problem. Nor need I solve the problem whether religious faith is the only factor which holds society together or whether more factors are involved: power, anxiety about civil war, ideological movements which have chosen the reproduction of their own group as a deliberate aim, and so on. I have been concerned with something else. The reason why I discussed the sociologists of religion in this section was not in order to solve their problems – for that I would need to be a professional, and I am not – but because we want to be shown what religious faith contributes to a society (the two questions were: is it indispensable and is it a factor of change?) to give us the starting point for an enquiry about the value of religious faith. The latter subject will be discussed in the next chapter. Here we can say that where religious faith is present – in whatever form, diluted or undiluted – it tends to consolidate the system. No matter what existing system we may have in mind here, religion shows the way into an existing symbolic universe, integrates the individual into it and in this way also works towards social cohesion and moral consensus. In empirical terms and seen from the continuation of the social and cultural system the function of religion is 'to make people want to do what they have to do anyway' (Wallace). As we will recall, that was precisely the reason why Marx had such a negative view of religion. That is understandable.

Who decides 'what people have to do anyway' and what is it? If that were established, it would make people ready to do what had to be done and not cause any problems. But it is not established. That makes religious faith, including Christian faith, in its indispensable function of consolidating a system, something which does not need so much control as the formation of political and social power. Otherwise religion makes people do wrong things. Meanwhile we must be aware that things have not gone wrong *because* religious faith makes people do them. They were already wrong, before – in schematic terms – faith came about. People who want to abolish religion because of their negative verdict on its function in consolidating systems must reflect that they will not make much progress unless they remove these wrong developments.

But here I am moving on to the next chapter. Who determines the truth of Christian faith and by what criterion?

7. *The value and truth of Christian faith*

As I have already pointed out, from the perspective of the sociology of religion it was obvious that we should look for the function of religious faith within a society. In other disciplines we come up against similar questions. For example a number of studies in the sphere of cultural or religious anthropology begin by making a functional connection between religion and society and arrive at the same results. De Waal Malefijt points out that everywhere and at all times religion, by means of beliefs, has had an ordering and stabilizing effect in 1. the organization of the family; 2. the support of the social order; 3. the foundation of the hierarchy; and 4. the development of economic organization. A quick look at our own society confirms this insight: religion, including Christian religion, makes an impact on all the four areas I have mentioned and not just through religious activities organized by the church. In other words, it is not only natural but also useful to test the phenomenon of religion against its actual social (economic organization) and political role (the foundation of the hierarchy) in a particular society.

Whether such a test is being carried out by the right method, whether the criteria by which the function or disfunction of religion are measured are correct, and so on are, of course, other questions. However, in the first instance these are questions which cannot be answered by theologians. There is no theological criterion for the practice of sociology and thus no theological criticism of sociology except when sociology allows itself to be led astray into statements which lie outside its professional competence; in other words, which do not follow from or support the empirical method practised by sociologists. However, the latter point emerges in two ways which are important for us. I shall investigate them first.

Theological criticism of statements by the sociologists of religion is possible and necessary where the functional approach of religion is presented as a functional explanation. This last is the case whenever religion is presented as a function of the social and cultural system. The word function can in fact be used in two senses: a social factor (for example religion) can *have* a function, but it can also *be* a function. Put schematically A → B → C. That means: B has a function in relationship with C (makes a contribution to C) but is a function of A (forms the contribution of A). In terms of our question: according to some sociologists of religion, religious faith makes a contribution to society (producing cohesion and consensus); according to others, in terms of its origin religious faith is to be derived from the socializing process itself. In the latter case we have functionalism in the strict sense of the word, in other words a functional theory which makes religious faith be a function rather than have a function. However, such a theory makes two mistakes: to infer from the functional requirement made of religious faith by society (being a precondition in the functional sense), namely that religion is a product or, to put it more attractively, a fruit of society, means that people then turn a functional relationship into a causal relationship, and transform society as a necessary condition for the existence (or continuation) of religious faith into a sufficient condition. Of course sociologists may do their best to try to explain religious faith (causally) and not just relationships (for example, functional relationships), but in that case they must use a different approach from a functional theory, since this can only demonstrate – it is not meant to do more – whether factor B (religion) is a contributory factor in the existence of factor C (society), and if so what it contributes. It does not explain anything.

Similarly: of course a society is a necessary condition for the existence of religious faith: if there are no people there is no religion. But the content of religious faith is always that there is something which transcends society, and to explain belief in that 'more' from the needs of society itself (the need for cohesion and consensus) is to confuse necessary and sufficient conditions and therefore amounts to knocking down an Aunt Sally. Why religion and where does it come from?

One example of such an explanation of religion in terms of society is Marx, as we have seen. Marx interpreted not only the value but also the truth of religious faith in functionalist terms and thus explained it away as an independent factor. The question is whether the functionalists among the non-Marxist sociologists of religion avoid these logical mistakes. There is always a risk of them: functional theories argue from the whole, from society, and assess the significance of faith for that whole in terms of the contribution which it makes towards the continuation of the whole. But they refrain from saying anything about the question whether the whole – society – must remain as it is or whether it must change. They do not express any value judgment on society. However, people with an interest in politics cannot leave things like that. For them it is only a small step to forgetting that this is a functional theory and begins from a value judgment on existing society. Marx did that quite frankly in a negative way; the bourgeois functional theories barely avoid the same thing at the opposite pole, passing a positive value judgment. Once a value judgment has been expressed about existing society, then an investigation in terms of the sociology of religion is no longer an investigation into the function of religious faith but an investigation of its instrumental value: the value or otherwise of Christian faith is measured by the contribution it makes to the realization of the ideal of society that people adopt.

I would see that as the pitfall of the functional approach to religion and society. I think that many Christians, above all if they have political interests, fall into this trap with open eyes (or rather, with closed eyes) and find it the most natural thing in the world for the value and sometimes even the truth of Christian faith to be judged by the degree to which it contributes to the realization of political and social ideals which people, including themselves, adopt. That means that in fact they allow values (and truth) to be prescribed by the social sciences, since these already determine what contribution faith makes, or rather does not make, to the realization of their political ideal. In this way the circle is closed: political ideals govern faith. What one first realized to be the 'wrong-headedness' of grandparents – the fact that they themselves could not see the way in which their faith was controlled by politics – now becomes a deliberate enterprise: belief has to demonstrate its value, and sometimes its truth, by its contribution to politics and society; in other words, the political and social ideal of a particular group. And so we arrive at something which was not intended: civil religion.

Does anyone not want to adopt that ideal if he or she is a Christian? Of course, but it is one thing to look for contributions which Christian faith can make to the support and the continuation of a society and a very different matter to measure the value and truth of Christian faith by the contribution that it makes to the society for which people struggle. At this point I shall not go into the fact that these ideals of society compete with one another but argue that one has *a priori* abandoned the independence of Christian faith once one measures its value (and truth) by its social and political significance. I am not saying that something of the sort cannot happen or may not happen, but in that case we have gone over to another kind of Christianity than can be seen as standing in the Christian tradition. Nor am I saying that Christians who are involved in politics are subordinating their faith to political ends; on the contrary, the one thing (religion) is not the other (politics). That will emerge later! I am simply indicating a pitfall into which Christians must not stumble. For the moment that is my sole concern.

As I have said earlier, a functional analysis can be confusing if people transpose the answer to the functional question to the level of value and truth; or, to put it in another way: function is not the same as intention. To interpret the relationship between religion and society in functional terms means not arguing from the meaning or intention that adherents to the faith express in their own view of faith and their practice of it but arguing from the actual effects that the existence of religious faith has on a society. Function and intention can coincide, but as Weber demonstrates in his *The Protestant Ethic*, which I have already mentioned, that need not be the case at all, and in fact is usually not the case. What a believing community aims to achieve with its faith and the actual effects of this faith are two different matters. The former is on the level of conscious thought and action: we get beyond that by analysing the doctrine. The latter is on the level of what can be calculated, measured and weighed, and here we use empirical investigation, going beyond the intentions of the agents. So all the time that I have been discussing the functional analysis of religious faith I have not been talking about the concern of human beings with their (Christian) faith but about what the effect of religious faith in fact is from the perspective of the question whether it contributes to the coherence of the whole. The difference between function and intention means that one can discuss the effects of religious faith on society at more than one level, in fact on three: 1. on the level of measurable effects; 2. on the level of the effects that adherents intend; and 3. on the level of the actual effect of their intentions.

To give an example: in the Christian tradition, on the basis of Romans 13.1-7, the authorities are seen as servants of God. What Christians intend by this doctrine of authority is a demonstration of why people owe obedience to the authorities (level 2).

According to Christians, the effect of this doctrine of authority is on the wane: even church members criticize the authorities and try to evade their control (for instance in tax avoidance) (level 3), while the measurable – social – effect is that Christians are usually faithful to the authorities, and are not easily roused to action, let alone revolution (level 1). I shall return to these three different levels when we consider the church (though in Part I we already came up against this difference of levels): do we mean the church as Christian doctrine has presented it (level 2, the ideal), do we mean the church as it falls short of the ideal which it has confessed in the past (level 3, the estimated realization of the ideal), or is it a matter of the quantifiable effects of the existence of a church or churches on the whole of a society (level 1: the reality controlled by scientific investigation)? In fact things are even more complicated because the Christian doctrine of the church (level 2) really consists of a multiplicity of views of the church which are so many ideals of being the church, varying from being extremely conservative to abandoning almost everything which recalls the church. But we shall consider that later. Here I shall be glad enough to have been able to make it clear that the purpose people envisage for the church, the significance they attach to it or the role they think that it should play in contemporary society – the functional theories about the relationship between religion and society – was not the real concern; that statements like 'Religious faith holds society together' do not mean that believers try to hold society together with their faith or see the significance of their faith in the fact that it consolidates systems and so on. All that – what people want their faith to do for society and where they are right in their wishes – is another matter and will be discussed in another Part.

Now it is time to sum up and ask, 'What is the farthest that we can go with the help of the sociology of religion?'

The first question for which we sought an answer was, 'Is religious faith a factor for change in a society?' In empirical terms this has a disappointing answer, at least for people who had hoped otherwise. Most authors I have mentioned come to the conclusion that religion serves to consolidate systems by socializing individuals, in other words integrating them into the existing universe of values and meaning. Socialization and identity are its fields of function (Drehsen). Religious faith therefore functions primarily and originally to maintain a society. From a sociological perspective faith is a factor of reproduction and in this sense reflects rather than changes a society. Even writers who want to see faith as a factor for change must concede that its actual effect is quite different from what was intended (Weber) or that at its best faith can produce either one thing or the other, stabilization or change. 'It is truly Janus-faced' (Lewy). To quote Mady Thung once again: if it is a factor for change it is not a particularly powerful one.

These are descriptive conclusions; in other words they reproduce the state of things and are (*a*) open to question through still more accurate investigation and (*b*) not normative. We can immediately say, 'That is the case, but things should be different!'

However, such a conclusion raises questions. If it need not be so, at least as far as Christianity is concerned – and that is what I have been about in using the word religion on these pages – why does the investigation so stubbornly show the same picture? Is (Christian) religion not capable – even in a derived sense – of bringing about change? And if that is the case is it because of believers themselves who fall short of this ideal of faith (teaching) or is it because of the actual content of their religion? Are all religions and churches the same here or does one religion have more elements which can further processes of change than the others?

The other question was, 'Can a society stand without religious faith and yet remain a society, or is religious faith a structural and functional requirement for any historically given society?' We have seen that one cannot say either yes or no, but that at most religious faith is one factor which produces social cohesion and moral consensus (and thus holds a society together) by integrating the individual into the whole and through the internalization of existing norms and values 'making him want to do what he has to do anyway', a process by which the individual in turn receives his identity. In the way, for example, in which earlier in the Christian church a person was only given a name – or was given a new name – when he or she was baptized.

This formulation first of all shows us that the dilemma 'Does religious faith have a function towards society or towards the individual?' cannot be a dilemma. Each function presupposes the other and especially sociologists like Weber, Malinowski and Parsons have already stressed that: the founding of community (as the conquest of anti-community, to use Nisbet's terms) and the giving of identity to the individual are two sides of one and the same thing. Philosophers (Hegel) and theologians (Pannenberg) make the same point from their perspective. A self is only a self if there are others which are not itself.

This formulation also makes it clear why religion, in its most extended form, is used so readily, so easily and in so many ways for political purposes. Insight into its functional contribution – socialization and identity – to the building up of a society can reduce its value to nothing (Marx). But we saw that modern Marxists are retracing their steps and attribute a relative autonomy to ideological arguments. Insight into the function of religion can clearly again increase its value. In any case, as experience demonstrates, those in power and those seeking power have a keen sense of the profits that religion, however vague, can produce. Here we need not just think of the military régimes in traditionally religious lands where the authorities usually take account of the existing religion when they are concerned to get consent to their exercise of power. New societies which deliberately distance themselves from religious faith (especially Christian faith) may again turn to religion (like the cult of Reason in 1789, or the Youth Movement in East Germany) as a factor which brings cohesion and consensus. Political authority (in the sense of exercising the right to power over others) clearly does not speak for itself nor is it accepted just like that by others. Seeking a religious foundation for making people do what they have to do anyway, subject themselves to the state (Rom.13.1-7), is not just a practice of the past. Modern revolutionaries do precisely the same and legitimate their power not with pragmatic considerations but with an appeal to religious myths: the people, the new man, freedom, and so on. Power over people must clearly be based on myths, so it produces new myths when the old ones are worn out. Religious faith is still experienced and accepted as being indispensable, even by people who find religion out of date.

We come to a last question: can religious faith be or become a critical authority over against society, if from a functional perspective it prolongs a historically given society? It is difficult to see how that could happen. Just as a form of society, specifically its political order, will suddenly come to an end, so in most cases faith comes to an end – and does so deliberately. But that happens in order to establish a new faith on the basis of which we can again require that faith still be critical towards this (new) society.

The question I am raising is not whether churches, as institutionalized religion, can also be critical of a society. Of course they can. We shall return to that later when we ask from where, in that case, the churches get their criteria for social and political criticism. What I am more concerned about here is the conditions for a critical church: if religious faith seems to prolong the society in which it appears, can it ever form a critical authority over against this society? The answer is that it can, because and in so far as religious faith also contains an element which distinguishes its adherents from the society to which they belong. In times of crisis – and I have been through many – a religion which establishes and prolongs the existing order seems to be aware of another, higher, order in which power, prestige and prosperity are not distributed as they are in the existing order. As I have already said, Durkheim can also be interpreted in this sense: we are not to respect the existing society; behind it will emerge the ideal society, and religion has further relevance there. In Durkheim, too, religious faith does not just serve as a consolidation.

How can that be? Because religion provides the individual with a double identity. On the one hand the identity of the individual is established in and through his or her being a member of society, which means that he or she gains an identity by internalizing the prevailing symbolic universe. For my purposes I shall call this horizontal identity. But the transcendent power which imposes obligations and comes through the existing pattern of values and norms is at the same time the power which is capable of demanding allegiance in a way which differs from all other social roles. That may be called vertical identity. In so far as religious faith can give experience of transcendence – but that is the critical question of 'religion in the religions' – religion is the authority which shows someone that he or she does not coincide with his or her social and political role. This makes possible a critical detachment from the existing society, its order, its values and its norms, on the basis of a religious faith which at the same time serves to consolidate that society. How this detachment is achieved is another matter, to which we shall return later.

This double identity (a person both coincides and does not coincide with society) is matched by a double conscience. On the one hand there is the obligation which compels the individual to fit into the pattern required by society, in short, being aware of what others expect of him or her. But by conscience we may also mean the reverse: the individual over against others. That is the way in which Socrates spoke about the conscience: it was his *daemon*, the voice of the other side which resounded in him and gave him courage to deal with others. That both forms of conscience stand side by side and cannot be played off against each other can be explained by the double identity which I described above.

I end this chapter with a conclusion: religious faith seems to be not only the mirror of a society; it can also create conditions for not coinciding with it as an individual. In this way religious faith can be a window as well as a mirror: it keeps open the sense that a society should be different. Thus in times of crisis religion can become a breeding ground for the self-criticism of a society.

I deliberately said breeding ground. Criticism needs criteria, and criteria for the social and political order do not come from religious faith but are taken up into it by making it a matter of faith. How that can be, and above all how it can be in such a way that faith is not made the locomotive for a political train, is something that I shall discuss in due course.

One more comment on belief as a breeding ground for self-criticism. There is a reason for this last word. Self-criticism is something different from the criticism of outsiders. Religious faith, including Christian faith, cannot put itself outside society. Total, radical criticism of society by Christians is not just criticism without criteria: it is cheap, easy and senseless to be a partner in the same undertaking and be derogatory about it.

8. Social determination and ideological criticism

It emerged in the previous chapter that Christian faith is not such a powerful factor for change in society as some commentators would have us believe. We shall now go a step further and see that Christian faith itself is involved in the historical process of change with all the questions which that involves for faith itself. Can it change without losing itself? Is what we believe today still the same as what the apostle Paul believed? I have discussed these and similar questions elsewhere. My conclusion was that in fact not all religions can survive (or indeed have survived) the process of historical change of which cultural history consists and that all the religions which have survived to the present need not, from a theological perspective, be good religions simply because they have survived. That is also true of Christian faith. It has to be proved that it is what it claims to be: a message of salvation for all people and therefore a universal faith. At this point I shall leave this aspect of things on one side and return to the process of change in which Christianity is also involved. That means that I am still occupied at the level of the sociological approach to faith. This chapter is above all about what one might call the sociology of Christian faith. I say that deliberately because there are some theologians who count a sociological explanation of faith – and of theology, as the next chapters will show – as part of theology. I am opposed to that. Theologians are not trained as sociologists nor for practising a sociology of Christian faith. If they nevertheless try, they can satisfy their universal human need to discover things, but that is not theology. It is not sociology either, but dilettantism.

The reason why theology needs sociological investigation is that faith is always faith in and sometimes of a particular society and also changes with this society. Sociological investigation draws attention to this fact (if the Christian church has not already done so itself) and in this way helps theology to think through the consequences of the historical and cultural determination of Christian faith as we know it and above all the correlation which seems to exist between changes in society and changes in Christian faith and to utilize them for the ongoing existence of church and faith.

I shall begin with an example: why must Christian religion today so necessarily be a factor for change? Because the changing of society is high on the list of priorities for a certain cultural level in Western Europe. Why does it have such a high position? Not because the Christian church has thought that society must be different. Nowadays you need not be a Christian to struggle for emancipation or for a juster society. More to the point, the Christian church did not begin this struggle, but Christians – though in not particularly large numbers – have slowly and somewhat sluggishly approved it. In practice that means that Christians are now going to their arsenal – Bible and tradition – to look for or forge weapons against racism, against pollution, against social exploitation, political enslavement, and so on. In this respect the Christian church is also changing with society.

One important fact in this connection is that the impulses come from elsewhere and not from the Christian churches themselves. Can we follow Rendtorff in saying that official Christianity as represented in the churches is being confronted with its own effects in European history (Enlightenment, humanism, Christianity outside the church) or must we maintain that people need not be Christians today or have been yesterday to know that strangers must be welcomed and the poor given their rights? I shall return to that in connection with general revelation.

Meanwhile the greatest problem connected with being involved in the process of change is not that changes mostly come from elsewhere and the churches follow but that precisely because the religious tradition of Christian faith comes to us from the past it is indissolubly bound up with past forms of society. The language and conceptuality in which the religious faith in and of a particular society is expressed, including Christian faith, reflect the normative value system applying in the society which in turn is indissolubly connected with the social and political organization of this society. A feudal, patriarchally orientated society speaks about God in male terms and in terms of absolute power. God is the one who can compel obedience and the human being is a vassal who must show obedience if he or she is not to be obliterated by God. So for instance we find in the Old Testament that God is the *baal* of humanity, the Lord who controls men and women and brings them to their senses by disciplining them. The man/woman relationship and the master/ servant relationship are reflected in religious faith. I note that fact here and leave out of account the problem of transference that is raised here for Christian faith. Can those who have abolished the feudal society, lords and all, still say Lord without getting an uncomfortable feeling (or no feeling at all) and should women sing hymns with predominantly male imagery from the church hymn books?

What we have begun to see here is that the Christian tradition of faith is not present in a pure state but is handed down to us in concepts and ideas which involve a particular social and political system. Here we come up against the problem of what for convenience I would sum up as the social determination of Christian religious concepts and conceptions. It not only relates to the conceptions and concepts of the Bible but involves the whole of the Christian tradition, up to and including the language of our parents who passed the faith on to us and in turn the language in which we hand it down to the next generation. But no one will or can claim that we must maintain the social system that comes down to us in Christian concepts and conceptions as a substructure of Christian faith: if it wants to be orientated on Christian religion, our society does not need to be composed of masters and slaves (Old Testament), to keep slaves (Paul), or – to go some way forward in history – to make society an organism in which high and low denote states in a natural order (Abraham Kuyper). On the contrary, we know very well that the message of Christian faith, from the Bible to the present day, can only be expressed in the terms of a particular time, and therefore that it is a prime requirement not to confuse the message and the time. If we do that, then not only the normative message of salvation, but also the social picture of a particular time with the help of which the message is put into words, is declared to be normative and we must require that if they want to become Christians, men must set themselves up as patriarchs, women must submit themselves to men, and so on. The examples can be multiplied and constantly confront us with the same question: how do we recognize the social determination of Christian concepts and how do we avoid imagining a political and social order – or parts of it – as being Christian, that is to say, as being commanded by God?

I use the phrase 'social determination of concepts and conceptions' because it has great advantages, compared with Marxist terms like class determination of thought and class consciousness, and at the same time does justice to the sociological insights which Marx provided. If we talk in terms of social determination of concepts and conceptions we need not go on to the slippery ice of Marx's basic philosophy, the starting point of which is that human consciousness is determined by the economic and social nature of humanity. Quite apart from its vagueness, this position is unverifiable and its explanatory power is nil. It explains everything and nothing. There is no reason whatsoever for assuming that talk about God is a product of social relationships. We have already seen that this is a form of criticism of religion which gives too much away: it criticizes by explaining away. The social determination of Christian concepts and conceptions does give an explanation, if only by making clear what it is that makes one person a victim and the other not. If we had to begin from class consciousness or socially determined consciousness, then that would remain unexplained, and even Marx himself could not explain it. Everyone would then be trapped in society. So it seems to me better to begin from the means of expression, in other words from the unavoidable fact that the only way in which people can possibly express themselves is in a language which involves a whole social and cultural system and that even now we cannot encounter the Christian message of salvation other than in this form. From this standpoint it is possible to make a tenable and convincing criticism of religious faith – including Christian faith – as this is found in a particular society and at the same time take that faith seriously or even adopt it.

The criticism which I intend here is usually called ideological criticism. Here ideology is any theory, doctrine or message which is used by those who advocate it to legitimate their own social or political privileges. Ideology is also used in a broader and more neutral sense to denote a theory (relating to politics or world-view) which is developed to organize people for a social end. The context usually makes it clear what concept of ideology is meant. If necessary, I shall also indicate it here.

Christian faith, like any other religion, is capable not only of functioning in its own right as an ideology – in the negative sense of the word – it also functioned and still functions as such in many spheres at many points. I have indicated the most important weak point already, the failure to recognize the social determination of Christian conceptions and concepts. At the same time this is where we find the key for specific criticism of ideology. Ideological criticism is usually practised by noting that the adherence to particular convictions serves the social interests of the adherents. But how does one demonstrate that? The argument is not an easy one. Interests can be misunderstood or ignored. Moreover, every individual and every group has interests. So having interests cannot be a criterion for ideological criticism. It is not having interests that makes faith an ideology: that happens when the interests cannot be justified. There are criteria for that: we need a normative view of society characterized by a fair distribution of obligations and rewards and a criterion for what is just and what is unjust action within this society. With the help of these two standards we can establish whether the social determination of Christian conceptions and concepts is recognized and an outdated picture of society itself is being included in the Christian message and giving it ideological features. In this way – through moral, social and ethical criteria – it seems to me that emancipatory criticism of religious faith, including Christian faith, is not only possible but also indispensable if faith is not to degenerate into social and political servitude which turns it into its opposite.

To sum up: Christian religion is not an ideology (in the negative sense), but the concepts which it uses can form part of an ideology because they are socially determined. We can discover if and when that happens by testing both the effects of Christian faith (which may be unintended) and its aims and the realization of these aims – here I return to the three levels that we distinguished in chapter 7 – with the help of moral, social and ethical criteria. In this way we can avoid entangling the view of society which has come down in the message of salvation with the salvation in the message itself.

In this approach we need not do violence to Christian faith as a religious phenomenon. It prolongs society in its own way. We harm it if we take too strong a line. I shall come back to this later in detail, but here without argument I shall simply claim that any society, because and in so far as it is a community, involves the conquest of anti-community (Nisbet). In this community individuals encounter salvation from God. Not all salvation, but salvation. Directed as they are (for this is 'the nature of the beast') to their fellow human beings and at the same time threatened as they are by the same fellow human beings (and also at the same time constituting a threat to others), they have society as the first form in which God encounters them with his salvation, giving them security (creating their identity) and putting them under obligation. The fact that religious faith prolongs society does not challenge the Christian religion, but it does not make it a religion in the negative meaning which the followers of Barth attach to the word. However, that is precisely what we would expect of Christian faith as faith in God's saving action.

Only if we do sufficient justice to this side of things can we also describe the way in which – and not just the conditions under which – a historical religious community like the Christian church has the chance to be critical towards a historical society without attacking itself as religious faith (by its own kind of prolongation). What is open to question and criticism is not the prolongation but what is prolonged. In fact the contradiction has always been there and still is. What we call secularization can be explained as follows: those areas are removed from the religion of the church in which the wrong things were stubbornly prolonged by the Christian church, 'wrong' meaning what was thought generally to hamper the freedom of members of a society to develop. By keeping an eye on what is prolonged, ideological use can be made of religious faith by individuals and groups and then it may transpire that the Christian church is caught up in the prolongation of unjust measures and political circumstances, or at least it may be asked whether that is the case. That happens wherever the Christian churches are self-satisfied and no longer willing to submit to the yoke of moral criticism (the universal human principles of humanity).

9. Contextual theology: politics in the outline proclamation of the Christian message of salvation

How far have we got in this Part? The Christian religion – institution-alized in the churches – is always the religion in or even of a particular society, wherever and whenever we encounter it. We must discover the empirical relationship between the two – who in fact does what with whom – from an empirical sociological investigation (chapters 5 and 6). However, we must not infer from the outcome of the investigation that the value and truth of faith are dependent on, because they are determined by, the contribution which that faith makes to the realization of political and social ideals – that would be a misunderstanding (chapter 7).

What we also learned from the investigation is that religious faith prolongs the society in which it functions: Christian faith also does that (even in its innermost being). But we must be careful that it does not prolong the image of society through the social determination of the Christian conceptions and concepts that comes with these ideas and concepts. That would give faith ideological features, recognizable through enslavement and the unnecessary domination of some by others (chapter 8).

In arguing like this I am putting the picture of society or, to be precise, political ideals, norms and directives, outside the real message of salvation presented by Christian faith – or rather, making it clear that they stand outside it. The saving message then has the meaning of the proclamation of God's salvation that is revealed in Jesus Christ. There is a positive relationship between Christian faith and politics or social welfare, but politics does not belong in this outline proclamation. By that I shall be indicating in the following chapters what the church thinks it must and may say about God's salvation which has appeared in Jesus Christ.

In saying this I am going against so-called contextual theology, and in the first instance against the trend in it which appeals to the context – what that is we shall see shortly – in order to legitimate its view that politics does belong in preaching. I do not mean 'going against' in a hostile sense but only that it does not seem to me to be a solution to the problem that this theology poses itself or at best is such a complicated solution that people have to have studied theology for years – very sophisticated, not to say mind-boggling theology – to be able to understand what is being said. I am not against this sort of theology when it is concerned with the praise of God but I am when, as in contextual theology, it has practical concerns. Complicated theology continues the teacher-pupil relationship. And we must not only not want to do that but not be involved in it. I have more doubts to mention: the contextual theology that I have in mind ends up solely in a theology of action (and action is then narrowed down to political action) and that seems to me to be one-sided. But here I have already gone too far into the theme of this chapter. Let me get back and begin in an ordered way.

What do I have in mind? Protest theology in general and specific forms of Latin American liberation theology in particular. Instead of protest theology I could also say political theology. Here I am not going to discuss theologies but in a rather broader sense set out the outline proclamations which seek to place politics and social criticism within the Christian message of salvation. There is much to be said for this. It is impossible for Christians to support political and social oppression and therefore it is impossible for theologians to produce a theology which legitimates social and political oppression. As this oppression seems to be connected with religious faith, including Christian faith, as a factor of prolongation – and it is that – it seems evident that the outline proclamation should be purged as far as possible of elements which confirm the *status quo* and involved as far as possible in social criticism. That is understandable not only in terms of content – which is what an outline proclamation is about – but also in personal terms: a theologian does not need to be the group ideologist of a society or of one part of it. If he or she wants to avoid that, then it is evident that in and with theology he or she is making a protest against society. Because this protest is meant to change society, even where it does not announce this aim, it is a form of political theology.

Being understandable and obvious is not the same thing as being tenable or full of promise. I shall not leave out protest – which is also why I am beginning with it – but I shall not make theology out of it. That is the point with which I am concerned. Throughout this book this position will also emerge from other perspectives, so that my conclusion will be that if it understood itself better, political theology would be not so much theology as social or political ethics.

This theology is called contextual because the context must be the legitimation of whether politics and social criticism get a place in the proclamation of the Christian message of salvation. What is meant by context or contextual?

The question calls for a complicated answer because 'contextual' uses context in two different meanings of the word which at first sight seem to be separate but which in contextual theology are so closely intertwined that they presuppose each other. On the one hand contextuality in theology is a matter of indigenization. Let us call that contextuality I. By this is meant that concepts and terms take on colour from their cultural context. To keep to colour: the Chinese Jesus is yellow and has slant eyes, the Jesus of blacks is black and the Jesus of whites is white with blue eyes. These are innocent pictures (or are they?). But a view of society is also involved here, and as we have seen that already leads to great complications. And what are we to think of Kuyper's remark that I quoted earlier: the yeast is the same but depending on the grain the bread is quite different? Is Kuyper really saying 'other bread'? How far can or may that be the same with Christanity? However, this difficult question is not relevant here.

Contextualization as indigenization of the Christian message of salvation appears in an explanatory context. The aim is to answer the question how it can be that Christians in black Africa regard, say, the resurrection of Jesus in such a different way from those in Latin America. Or they may also look at Jesus in a different way from their cultural neighbours without departing from the norm of Christian faith, and how far they may go in this direction is something that theology must investigate. Contextuality in the sense of indigenization is a form of sociology of faith and theology. It is described and explained, not judged and justified. Each theologian reflects in his or her theology the cultural context in which he or she operates – and that includes the social context: that is important.

The real complication is to come, but first let me mention another concept of contextuality: theology must (and this is now a requirement) be contextual in the sense of alluding to local, regional or even continental forms of social and political oppression. For the moment I call that contextuality II. This, taken by and large, is the concept of contextuality which is used or at least presupposed by political theologians: a theology says nothing if it has not included in its outline proclamation the social or political context of its own country, people or area, in the sense that it seeks to change the context by means of opposition to exploitation and oppression. In this form of words I note once again how clearly contextual theology (contextuality II) constructs itself as the opposite of theology which produces prolongation. It stands or falls with the protest against the traditional political and social order. Hence in countries where there is more political protest than elsewhere political theology flourishes, and in countries where there is less political protest such protest must seem to be almost artificial if it seeks to be the *raison d'etre* for political theology. The complication to which I referred is that the word context is often used with both meanings interchangeably, sometimes innocently, and sometimes as a theoretical conjuring trick.

As to the first point: anyone who looks at a Chinese print of the child Jesus will find it disturbing and regard it as contextuality I. That also goes for Pieter Breughel's portrayal of the census in Luke 2: the picture has Jesus born in the Flemish countryside. So we say that it is contextuality I. But is that so certain? Is there not a form of annexation, albeit naive, if Jesus is portrayed as Flemish or Chinese? Why do we no longer smile if Jesus is portrayed as a white, blue-eyed Westerner but then suddenly say that you can make anything of Jesus if you leave out the fact that he was a Jew? If that is a valid counter-argument against white – e.g. Germanic – contextuality (I) then it is also an argument against yellow and black Jesuses. Unless we meant that Jesus may indeed be black or yellow but not white, at least not a particular kind of white. But in that case there must clearly be a reason for thinking that and the reason cannot consist in anything other than a criterion with the help of which we can judge whether conceptions belong in context I or context II, in other words, whether they shift from context as an unavoidable fact (the cultural determination of any theology) to context as a subject of dispute and change (every theology may be required to oppose political or social oppression). Where do we get the criterion from? I shall return to this shortly. First I must finish the subject I have been talking about. For contextual theology thus seems to mean two things which can overlap. To put it with the help of similar-sounding terms for the sake of clarity, it is said on the one hand that it is the inescapable fate of theology to be socially determined (contextuality I) and at the same time that it has the task of challenging social determination. The big question is of course how this can happen: how can people whose fate it is to be socially determined in their thought and action at the same time be so free of social determination that they can challenge society? I shall now narrow contextuality to social and political context and then in due course I shall widen it again.

The solution offered by Marxists in discussions is to divide the two contextualities carefully between themselves and bourgeois ideologies. They saddle the bourgeois ideologies with contextuality I, social determination as an unavoidable fact: they cannot be anything but class-determined thought. However, when they are talking about themselves social determination disappears and all that is left is contextuality II: the praxis of the revolutionary which changes the context. Political theologians can also work in this way. According to Dorothee Sölle there are two kinds of theology: that of the prosperous citizen who in his social captivity thinks only of safeguarding his own interests and therefore does not want any change in society, and that of people who turn against exploitation, oppression and violence and therefore challenge existing society. My description is meant to convey two things. In the first place this approach is not free from self-satisfaction and indeed smugness. I have never met anyone who worked with this twofold divison and put himself or herself among the sinners. Sölle too counts herself on the good side, not among the citizens enslaved by self-interest. But – the in second place – she does not explain how she belongs to a society which is trapped in bourgeois thought and at the same time can see through and challenge this society. She is simply following the 'findings' of popular Marxist theory. So this is a bad finding in two ways: it does not explain anything and it leads a respectable theologian like Sölle to ingenuous self-praise.

If contextuality is such a complicated concept, how can we use it in theology? Does it help us to see more clearly what needs to be seen and say more clearly what has to be said? I shall answer this question in two stages. The first part of the answer will consist in an investigation of what contextuality (both I and II) actually presupposes. In the second part I shall above all raise questions about its application.

I can be brief about contextuality (with the stress on I) after what I have already said: the term in fact serves as a description and explanation of plurality within theology and Christianity and at the same time as a challenge to the churches to take account of it in their dealings with one another. It cannot legitimate plurality. As long as no criteria are given for establishing the limits of plurality or, in the opposite direction, the limits of Christian identity, one cannot appeal to it. In that case everything is as good – or as bad – as everything else.

Contextual theology (the accent is now on context II) in fact comes close to theology which includes political and social action in the outline proclamation and legitimates this somewhat unusual embellishment of theology with a reference to the social and political context which calls for such embellishment. Does that programme for action and its directives in fact arise out of the context? Can contexts, consisting of social and political situations which have grown up through history, make demands ? No, contexts never do that and anyone who thinks that they do makes a mistake not in terms of subject-matter but theologically. To begin with the latter: to present historical situations or events as authorities which have the power to command is to want to read the divine commandment out of history. But that can be done only in a quite arbitrary way and always amounts to an uncontrollable identification of one's own plans with God's will. The history of Christianity shows the catastrophic consequences of such identifications (Adolf Hitler welcomed by the German Christians as an intervention by God to rescue Germany). In terms of subject-matter the mistake is no less great: 1. Contexts call for directives for action but do not offer them. 2. Where the context does call for a directive the assessment of this context depends on the theologian concerned. However, criteria and normative ideas about people and society are needed for judging social and political situations. 3. Thus in contextual theology (contextuality II) normative ideas precede theology itself. They are what makes the demand and not the context. 4. In other words, it is not the context that legitimates the programme of action offered by political theology but the normative ideas of humanity and society which these theologians adopt. 5. So theology does not get a chance to work; social-philosophical and social-ethical criteria determine the virtue and acceptability of political and social ideas. 6. Where theology is involved here is to provide legitimation for already chosen convictions and to motivate others to approve these convictions. This last function need not be illegitimate, but I shall keep the question for later. The only thing I would say here is that of course you cannot offer religious legitimation in order to avoid a discussion!

With this analysis I have shown what contextual theology in fact presupposes *qua* political theology: it is a political theory of action which works with theological arguments. This makes its construction complicated and sometimes leads it to sail close to the wind when it comes to the question: does God will what we will or do we will what God wills? I think that liberation from social and political oppression can be commended by much simpler theories for political and social action and must not, may not – and that also means need not – be burdened with the theological arguments of contextual theology which become more sophisticated the longer they go on. What I have indicated here with steps 1 to 5, the actual steps which contextual theology undertakes before it begins on theology, should be enough. Here liberation movements can not only be sufficient in themselves; they are also much better without it. That should also be enough for Christians. They approve what is good, as I shall demonstrate in subsequent Parts, and they do so because they believe that the criteria for that also come from God.

The question remains how contextual theology – Sölle was the example – can fall within the context as an inescapable fate (context I, social and cultural captivity) and at the same time can have the insight, knowledge and openness to develop a theology which sees through and disputes this context (contextuality II). Where then does the knowledge and insight of this theology come from? The answer is that this theology begins with itself. It has learned from Karl Barth that it may. But unlike Barth it then refers to experience.

To make this position clear, I shall begin with context as indigenization (context I). On the one hand (and usually) we meet it as a process of unconscious assimilation. Whatever culture Christianity enters, it is more or less stamped by this culture. In this form indigenization is as old as Christian faith itself. In the past Western Christianity showed a great deal of misunderstanding over this phenomenon: (*a*) Western religious patterns were imposed: (*b*) Western indigenization itself was not recognized; and (*c*) in the theological sphere – especially on the Reformation side (Barth, Kramer) there was even condemnation of such forms of assimilation.

However, indigenization can also be undertaken deliberately. In that case it is a programme which aims at restoring identity that was repressed by colonial expansion (by the West in the case of the Third World, by men in the case of women, and so on). Here it is a matter of going back not only to the old popular culture (roots) but also to the religion of the fathers (or mothers). The context from which people were driven out (context I) and to which they are now returning is the area where blacks, women, basic groups, the poor, revolutionaries and so on can again live out their own experiences, as they could not earlier because society was colonialized by males, the rich, the violent and so on. The new possibility arises where and when the occupier is driven out. So now we have black theology, feminist theology, grass-roots theology and so on, all theologies which appeal for their own particular content to their contextual experience.

As a model by which I can demonstrate precisely what happens I have taken North American black theology, which is not to be confused with the black theology of Africa (there are as many black theologies as there are white). 'Black' is black identity ('black is beautiful') and black theology is ultimately concerned for a theology (outline proclamation) in which justice is done to black identity. But that justice has to be won: black is at the same time anti-white, opposition to the context of alienation and oppression within which people live; indeed one only arrives at 'black' as an experience of one's own identity through opposition to white domination and therefore anti-white gets priority in the outline proclamation. We could put it another way: the anti-white element in the outline proclamation (the programme of opposition) – contextuality in the second sense – derives its justification from black identity as a contextual experience (context in the first sense).

This model is instructive because – ultimately – it shows how the question which we left to one side must be solved, the question of how it can be that social and political dependence is an unavoidable fate and yet with a theology – I took Sölle as an example – one can escape it and be in a position to see through and challenge society. How that can happen is now clear: people refer to the contextual experience of women, blacks, the poor and so on as their own approach to reality, their own source of knowledge. In the most literal sense you begin with yourself. A Marxist confronted by the same dilemma cannot do that. He is in a void. But religious people can do it. Beginning with yourself is beginning with God, not because you are God, but because your own authentic experience is a new medium for reality (viz. God) to disclose itself. However, if I am justified in beginning with myself it is no longer nonsense to claim that captivity is a necessary fate (for others), but that I can escape it. If Sölle means it that way, her comment about good and bad theology is more understandable. However, whether she then becomes less haughty is another question. And yet another question is whether contextual theology can appeal for its subject matter in this way to contextual experience. I shall make a couple of remarks which are meant as question marks.

First, who establishes, with the help of what criterion, where the context begins and where it ends, how narrow or how broad it is, in short, what shall serve as a context which provides contextual experience? Is colour of skin a criterion? Or sex? Or are shared collective norms and values? Or ethnic affinity? Must we think of a region? But in that case where does it begin and end? And are all the people who dwell in this region part of it, so that all experience counts, or does only that of some people count? Until there is an answer to these questions the concept of context and therefore of contextual experience is in a void and there is every chance that contextual experience simply means the experience of a group of like-minded people.

That brings me to a second comment. Some years ago Oene Bult appealed in the *Leewuarder Courant* for Friesian identity. So is there a Friesian God as well as a black one? I do not mean this as a joke but as an approach to the following question. Does every context produce its own God? That would mean that we had returned to a pre-Jewish stage. Israel had got so far as confessing the one God, albeit simply for one people. The apostle Paul had to go beyond that with his preaching of justification through Jesus Christ to make it clear that this one God is the universal God in the sense of being God of and for all people. If the context prescribes what is God's revelation and command, the context becomes God. Contextual gods are the obsolete gods of paganism. Therefore there were as many gods as there were contexts. One God and Father of all means that contexuality of experience is a form of tribalism (Jenkins), an unavoidable handicap but one to which the Christian church can never succumb.

The third comment is that to begin from experience rests on a misunderstanding. Experience is at the same time interpretation, and for interpretation a framework of interpretation is needed within which the experience can have a place, in other words, mean something. That also applies to the experience of faith. Who or what people experience of God depends on the search pattern that they use. You can only cry, 'Here he is again' (van Peursen), if you have first had an indication of who he is. Without such an indication anything that makes an impression can be God, from fertility up to and including feminine emotionalism. So what does the appeal to experience mean? That is a question that we must certainly raise here. With the help of the Christian search pattern 'here he is again' do we 1. refer to a place where we did not expect him at all, or 2. make a new search pattern? Of course the latter is possible; who could rule that out? But if by experience we mean Christian experience of God, then a definite response to the Christian search pattern is necessary.

The fourth comment sums the others up. As I said earlier, the appeal to contextual experience expresses a concern to find a legitimate place in the outline of the Christian message of salvation for women's struggle against a male culture, the struggle of blacks against their colonial rulers, the struggle of the poor (or rather of those who regard themselves as their champions).

Now what I finally want to assert goes back to what I said about contextual theology as political theology: women, the poor, blacks and so on rightly point to experiences (more about them in due course), but the struggle of women, of blacks and so on does not derive from the context and is not a contextual experience but is based on normative ideas about man and woman, white and black, rich and poor and so on. Without these normative ideas there would be no experience of justice, alienation or domination. That such experiences do have a place is based on at least some sense of this. Women – to focus on them for the moment – may have these normative ideas today and fight for their share in implementing them. To repeat what I have already said, no theology is needed for that, no attempt to cram being a woman or being black into the Christian message of salvation. What is needed is a sense of justice and injustice and the application of these normative concepts to forgotten, alienated or underprivileged groups. A theology of doing not only burdens the dispute with all kinds of unnecessary and complicated theological questions but also leads to wrong theology, to a theology which – I might almost say – has made so much of a clean sweep of creation and salvation in creation that everything now has to be brought into the eternal salvation which appeared in Jesus Christ. The following chapters should show that normative ideas can be Christian even without being derived from the message of salvation.

I now end with two conclusions. The first begins with a question. Is contextual experience then nonsense from a theological point of view? Not at all. Christian theology cannot do without it for its outline proclamation. But it needs it in the sense that contextual experiences, of say women, blacks, and the poor, can disclose and bring to the fore elements in the Christian search pattern for God which were snowed under and would not have been rediscovered without the experience of being a woman or being black. Moreover, there seems to me to be a remarkable paradox. Contextual theology is concrete theology, relating to people in a region. That does not seem to me to be open to contradiction. But precisely because theology (an outline proclamation) is not only contextual and concrete but is also the vehicle for a wealth of themes which are not specific and concrete, we can have something like a contextual rediscovery. A generation which has never learned the whole tradition – 'the whole bag of tricks', as Graham Greene put it – but only contextual truths and commandments will never be a generation that makes contextual discoveries.

This recognition, moreover, has a critical side. Contextual experience in the sense that I have just mentioned, the experience for example of women or blacks, does not mean that we now have to imagine our God as being a woman, or envisage a black God or a black Messiah. In that case we would again be wide of the mark. Contextual experience results, rather, in a criticism of the one-sided way in which the limited and limiting world of experience of men and whites has come into the service of the gospel of salvation. We can only speak of God with the help of socially determined conceptions and concepts. Why then only conceptions and concepts from the world of masters and not from that of servants, from men and not from women? Contextual experience works as a kind of permanent revolution within the Christian outline of belief in God: it compels us to adjust this outline so that God is named not only in terms with which males or rich people or whites can identify, but in terms with which everyone can. God is not the God of some but the God of all, so he must be spoken of by the Christian church in such a way that he can be recognized by all.

My second conclusion is that contextuality is a term which can be used in a much more meaningful way in connection with the church than it can in connection with theology. The outline proclamation of God's salvation in Jesus Christ cannot so easily be made contextual: on the contrary, it is one of the most essential features of salvation that it transcends all contexts. But the Christian church cannot exist other than contextually. It is not just the church in or even of a society, but society is its inevitable fate: it does something with the Christian church. And at the same time society is its task: the Christian church does something with this society. In political and social terms, too, this society is a challenge: the poor must be raised up from the mire, the oppressed freed from alien domination, the black and coloured extracted from the humiliation of apartheid. All that must happen, and Christian faith regards it as a matter of faith that this is a divine commandment. However, the church must also remain itself. The church *qua* church cannot take part in the power struggle that goes with politics. That will become clear in due course. Nor is preaching commitment to the poor a matter of saying *how* that must happen. For that, planning based on social ethics, social philosophy and politics is necessary. All that must happen, but it is not the only thing that the Christian church does with society;

it is not doing what it alone can do, passing on the message of God's salvation that has appeared in Jesus Christ.

Are there then two things in the preaching of the church? Yes indeed: there is the message of salvation, which I have called the outline proclamation, and what must be made a matter of faith in the context: directives and norms for political and social salvation.

Action as a matter of faith is not the same thing as a theology of action. The Christian church needs more to be a contextual church than simply theology. If we do not recognize that, our theological outlines will be as stuffed full as those of contextual theology. In order to be able to function contextually, society has to be analysed. Theology cannot do that. So the church must set its light alongside the social sciences and social philosophy. In these areas theologians can only repeat what they are told or be interlopers. Analysis of normative ideals, principles and directives is also needed. For that the Christian church must go elsewhere and not to theology.

Is theology, then, interesting to young people and the study of theology attractive to them? Certainly theology is not the most important discipline for the practice of politics and social criticism, but that is not necessarily a bad thing. I can illustrate what I mean from a theologian who, confronted with the poverty of a Brazilian industrial city, said, 'I could not do much in this situation with my theology', and then tried to develop his theology (i.e. his outline proclamation) in such a way that there was a place in it for opposition and rebellion against the social and political order. That cost him a good deal of hard thinking which would not have been necessary had he realized in time that theology is not the usual means or instrument for liberation from social misery and political oppression. If we want a strategy for rebellion and opposition to oppression, we must go somewhere other than theology.

To end: as a church in and of a society, the Christian church needs more than just the proclamation of Jesus Christ. It also has in a general way to commend directives for social and political salvation. It has not discovered these itself, but they belong to what the Christian church has to say. The two elements in the proclamation of the church do not coincide, must not be confused, cannot be played off against each other and come from one and the same God. But that already takes us towards the next Parts.

Bibliography

P.L.Berger and T.Luckmann, *The Social Construction of Reality*, Allen Lane, The Penguin Press 1966

J.Bowker, *The Sense of God*, Oxford University Press 1973

T.Campbell, *Seven Theories of Human Society*, Oxford University Press 1982

K.W.Dahn, V.Drehsen and G.Kehrer, *Das Jenseits der Gesellschaft, Religion im Prozess sozialwissenschaftlicher Kritik*, Munich 1975

G.Dekker, *De mens en zijn Godsdienst*, Bilthoven 1975

A.De Waal Malefijt, *Religion and Culture*, Collier-Macmillan 1968

E.Durkheim, *On Morality and Society. Selected Writings*, edited and with an introduction by Robert N.Bellah, Chicago University Press 1973

F.Engels, *Anti-Dühring*, Lawrence and Wishart 1955

H.Falding, *The Sociology of Religion*, London 1974

D.E.Jenkins, *The Contradiction of Christianity*, SCM Press 1971

R.L.Johnstone, *Religion in Society. A Sociology of Religion*, Prentice-Hall, Engelwood Cliffs ²1983

L.Kolakowski, *Religion*, Oxford University Press 1982

H.M.Kuitert, 'Contextueel of academisch? Op zoek naar relevante-theologie', *Gereformeerd Theologisch Tijdschrift* 83, 1983, 188-203

G.Lewy, *Religion and Revolution*, Oxford University Press, New York 1974

K.Marx, *The German Ideology*, Lawrence and Wishart 1965

H.Moritz, 'Religionssoziologie als theologische Disciplin', *Theologie und Leben* 95, 1970, 881-92

A.W.Musschenga, 'Godsdienst: ideologie of ideologiekritiek', in *Segmenten, Studies op het gebied van de theologie*, edited for the Faculty of Religion at the Free University of Amsterdam by T.Baarda, H.M.Kuitert, G.N.Lamens, and P.L.Schram, I, 1978, 101-56

R.Nisbet, *The Social Philosophers. Community and Conflict in Western Thought*, Heinemann Educational 1974

T.Rendtorff, *Gesellschaft ohne Religion*, Munich 1975

M.Schoffeleers, *Pentecostalism and Neo-traditionalism. The*

Religious Polarization of a Rural District in Southern Malawi, Anthropological Papers of the Free University of Amsterdam 1, Amsterdam 1985 Seminar, *Religion und gesellschaftliche Entwicklung*, Frankfurt 1973

J.Skorupski, *Symbol and Theory. A Philosophical Study of Theories of Religion in Social Anthropology*, Cambridge University Press 1976

P.Smits, *Godsdienst en kerk in het licht an der sociologie*, The Hague 1972

Mady Thung, *The Precarious Organization: Sociological Explorations of the Church's Mission and Structure*, Religion and Society Series 5, Mouton, New York 1976

A.Wallace, *Religion. An Anthropological View*, Random House, New York 1966

M.Weber, *The Protestant Ethic and the Spirit of Capitalism*, Allen and Unwin 1977

T.Weber, 'Politische Autorität und Revolution', *Zeitschrift für Evangelische Ethik* 20, 1976, 98-113

Monica Wilson, *Religion and the Transformation of Society*, Cambridge University Press 1971

III God and Society

10. The empty world

What is this Part about? That has already been prepared for by the decisions made in the previous Parts. Politics and social criticism are not theology (thought of as an outline proclamation of the Christian message of salvation). Ultimately this conclusion depends on how we think of the involvement of God with politics and the social order. Is God only criticism of this order? Is there something of God's new creation in the social and political order? – those are just a couple of questions.

How did previous generations of Christians think about this and from what presuppositions do I myself begin? That is what Parts III and IV will basically be concerned with. This means that we are now engaging in theology. Of course this is a bird's eye view of theology, or better, theology restored to what in my judgment is indispensable for the understanding of the contemporary discussion over faith and politics, but it is nevertheless theology. I have schematized where schemes seem to me to be useful; presented trends by way of a model where that has advantages for understanding; and drawn a historical line where I want to show how one theological question raises another and how that often means that the limelight is no longer occupied by the problem which has to be solved but by the answer which people want to rescue. However, answers must not be rescued. That is an unscientific attempt (the important thing is not my answer but the truth) and in any case gets us nowhere, even in theology. Fortunately things are not always like that, nor need they be always like that. Theological questions are often very meaningful and the answers to them can in turn be an occasion for new meaningful questions. But that is only half the story. New theological questions do not come up immediately. Usually something happens outside the sphere of theology – in church or society – which makes earlier solutions doubtful. We shall see that the chain of questions which I shall discuss in the two chapters in this Part are linked precisely according to this process.

How do believers – Christians, churches, theologians; each term applies here – imagine the relationship between God and society (as a social and cultural system)? With this question we have left behind an approach from outside and Christianity itself is speaking. It believes and confesses something when it talks about God and society. On the one hand that puts things sharply: they can now become matters of faith. On the other hand it also relativizes: believers, too, are people and what they say about the world above comes from below. It can seem something very like absolutism to realize that at times.

So we are concerned with society and its social and political order: I am focussing the question on this. According to Christianity, is God also involved there in the sense that there is a divine will for politics and the social order? In fact according to the overwhelming majority of Christians and theologians that is the case. However, the way in which we take note of this will is imagined in different ways. The oldest and simplest theological construction is that of theocracy. The literal meaning of this term (*theos* is the Greek word for God) is the rule of God, and that indicates precisely what is meant by it: society is regulated, ruled by God himself. Here 'regulate' means that God himself (*a*) gives the laws for society; (*b*) gives them through the spiritual ministries of priests, prophets and other mediators; and (*c*) gives them for all aspects of society from the state as an institution down to and including the family. Classical models of theocracy are Israel in the period described by the Old Testament, Islam, and much more recently – and at the same time in a less fundamental way – Geneva under the régime of Calvin. However, not only in the past but also today Christians still have theocratic ideals, although in their case we may say that these are ideals which are called such by their creators (for example van Ruler), whereas in reality all they have in common is that the political order is imagined as being initiated by God. But the role of mediators (in Geneva the preachers threatened to become that) has disappeared.

In classical theocracy, however, the role of the mediator is essential: the mediators represent God, they have knowledge of what God wants and they are responsible for jurisprudence to implement this will if there is uncertainty or difference of opinion over it. That means that the mediators – whatever office they may hold – have unassailable authority: they give the law, pronounce judgment and have executive power with God as their absolute backing. There is no higher appeal. Where that leads to is described in detail by V.S.Naipaul in his book *Among the Believers*, and if we have not seen the book we have read it in the newspapers: what Naipaul describes is Iran under Ayatollah Khomeini and his religious aides. The subjects are powerless when faced with the authority and have no rights in any difference of opinion over it.

The social and political presuppositions from which theocracy begins are that the people is one, the people believes and the people obeys God. Put in everyday terms, only where church and people coincide can theocracy exist. Societies where these presuppositions are not present can only live with a political order on a theocratic basis through force. We must therefore take the theocratic ideals of a number of Dutch Reformed theologians from the previous century and the beginning of this century with a pinch of salt. They saw few or no political implications for their thought and limited theocracy to a dream in which church and people again coincided in the Netherlands. But the more a country is unchurched the less room there is for theocratic dreams. The theological conditions for a theocracy are as outdated as the political and social conditions: revelation from God does not happen in the form of communications of God's will for society. There is no theology which would want to maintain that.

Moreover we see that where theocracies exist they tend to disappear again in more or less quick time. *If* God gives directives for politics and society, he certainly does not do so by making his will known directly to his servants.

The so-called doctrine of the two kingdoms became much more important. Without writing a history of it here, I can easily demonstrate that the political conditions for the rise of a doctrine of two kingdoms were rather more favourable. It presupposes that church and people – in contrast to the dream of theocracy – do not coincide and that therefore a Christian is concerned not just with the church and its gospel (the spiritual kingdom) but also with the state and it ordinances (the secular kingdom). Such a historical constellation forms the breeding ground of the doctrine of the two kingdoms:

Augustine wrote his *City of God* at a time when throne and altar were at odds with each other. By way of a small digression: the description of the time since Constantine the Great as a time in which throne and altar coincided – this description comes from Moltmann – needs to be corrected. The situation was much more complicated than that. At all events, a doctrine of two kingdoms is unnecessary if the church coincides with the state.

What is the relevance of the doctrine of the two kingdoms for the question of the relationship between God and society, with its political and social order, which concerns us here? I am aware that this doctrine has other and more far-reaching aspects, but I shall return to them in a separate chapter. Here I shall keep to my plan and discuss the doctrine of two kingdoms because and in so far as it is the model for a particular approach, as was theocracy.

But that is not all. In the classical doctrine of the two kingdoms God guides people not only with his will for society but also with his grace. Alongside the doctrine of general revelation, from ancient times there has been that of general or restraining grace, which has to explain why a society existed and could exist in a world distorted by sin and guilt. The answer is, briefly, that the society itself is, so far as it exists, a form of grace, or in modern language a form of salvation. The classical doctrine of the two kingdoms was about both directives and salvation. Both come from God, who as creator is present in society, informing it and preserving it through created reality.

We do not need to go any further at present with the doctrine of the two kingdoms. It represents an elegant solution to the question who or what may be regarded as the supplier of directives for political and social action: the created world itself, which is open to anyone who uses his or her understanding, but through this created world ultimately God, who has given it his order and who preserves it wherever and whenever this order is still maintained in some way.

The next step – but now I am also being a historian and not concerned with models – is the discovery that nothing may be called natural or an order of creation. The things to which the Christian church gave this name – from marriage to political order – did not exist 'from creation' but seem to be a product of a historical development and are still constantly changing. With this discovery of the historical character of what people had previously called orders of creation – as the result of historical investigation – the bottom falls out of the doctrine of two kingdoms. Of course there is still a duality, just as there was previously: the world (really society) and how to live in it on the one hand and the message of the gospel on the other. But this world is now secularized (the term comes from Troeltsch): it is empty as far as God is concerned since the investigation has demonstrated that the so-called proofs of God are not proofs at all. The doctrine of two kingdoms is from that moment on elaborated in a new way. The duality is now that of the world on the one side, with its own social and political problems which we must try to solve in as practical a way as possible, while on the other there are human beings as persons, also with their own demands that they should be able to become persons in an empty world, a requirement which is met by the Christian message of the gospel: it anchors human beings in God, in a reality beyond history, and therefore puts them in a state of continuing to remain in history (the empty world).

This secularization of the doctrine of the two kingdoms therefore seems to have enormous consequences. In the 'empty world' the human being remains the only point at which God and the world make contact. This changes the concept of revelation radically in both form and content. If the human person is the only funnel through which revelation can be received, there is no way for revelation other than going through this being a person. Revelation becomes Word and nothing else. However, where this Word comes from remains obscure. It cannot come from history, since no revelation comes from there. So the Word is unhistorical. But what is an unhistorical Word? And how do we know that it is the Word and not human words? Can I just reply, 'I'm sure of it and that is enough'? A whole generation of theologians took the side of this theological personalism (Gloege) which for its own part – though it speaks for itself – could show little interest in questions about the political and social order and was more interested in the question how I rescue myself *from* the grasp which the ordinances now have on human beings. But I shall not enlarge on this. Let us return to the secularization of the doctrine of the two kingdoms. I would make two points here.

The first is that it explains how the doctrine of the two kingdoms could get such a bad name. The construction of the duality does not necessarily lead to the fact that on the one hand the public sphere comes into existence with autonomous areas of economy, social institutions and the political order and on the other hand there is personal life, not autonomous but regulated by the Christian tradition of faith, hope and love; however, it can get there very easily. The vulnerability of this duality (which is what it is, as we shall see later) does not lie so much in the term 'autonomous'. That means that the economic order is rather different from a marriage and that you must resolve economic or political conflicts in a different way from marriage conflicts. So 'autonomous' does not mean above moral assessment. Friedrich Naumann, whose name is indissolubly connected with this autonomy, never made this last assertion. He merely said – and it seems very plausible – that the control of political, social or economic action needed to happen with the help of other criteria than Christian love of neighbour.

Of course autonomy can also suggest a moral and even immoral action. However, that is a construction which seems to have left behind even the appearance of a doctrine of two kingdoms, so I shall leave it on one side.

My second comment is that a secularized worldly realm where norms prevail but without relation to God is a thought which Christians do not find it easy to arrive at. What we then see happen is an attempt to save what is to be saved by presenting the actual orders as orders of God. The world is 'empty' and must remain so: revelation has no other funnel than the person. Yet at the same time it is clear that the norms for the social and political order cannot be left in the air but must also come from God. But how can the two starting points coincide without becoming rivals? Emil Brunner, a contemporary of Karl Barth, entangled (or ensnared) himself in this problem in his book *Das Gebot und die Ordnungen* ('The commandment and the ordinances'). There is an authentic will of God (das Gebot), the commandment which becomes clear to us in an encounter with the God who speaks (the unhistorical Word) and in terms of content looks for an act of sacrificial love which transcends all moral norms and orders, even doing away with them. Alongside that there is the will of God as it comes to us in the ordinances, to which Christians are also obedient because they come from God, though they do not reach them as the commandment does: as an actual demand of the God who himself speaks in a specific situation.

The problems into which this pattern leads concern above all the hierarchy of commandment and ordinance: what has precedence when and for what reason? And the answer to this question, if one can be given, again raises all kinds of problems. But I shall leave those on one side. The starting point of the argument was that the world cannot really be 'empty'. Brunner's solution lay in distinguishing between the personal love commandment and the *de facto* ordinances relativized through the commandment. His conception of things became popular in both Europe and America, even where he was not mentioned by name. At its deepest, Christianity is really personal love and altruism, but the ordinances are also part of it.

In the meantime we should not forget that the doctrine of two kingdoms still has its propagandists, even in its classical elaboration, especially among conservative Lutherans like Althaus, Elert and Künneth. The last mentioned – like Thielicke – speaks of 'ordinances of preservation' and not of ordinances of creation. In this way general revelation and general grace are summed up in one term: God is needed not only to provide an ultimate foundation for the ordinances (general revelation) but also to explain the continuance of a sinful world (general grace). We may approve the concept of faith behind the two notions but we may not approve the construction under which they are brought – 'ordinances of preservation'. These 1. explain a particular phase of a historical course as being not just 'natural' or of the 'order of creation' but as the 'order of preservation', and 2. do that – and can only do that – in an arbitrary way; for example, why are property and work divine ordinances and not trade unions? 3. As a rule they do it in forms which are no longer applicable, not framed in terms of a society like ours. To give an example of the last point: it is no longer appropriate in our modern industrial society to identify work, as used to happen, with a calling, and calling with vocation by God. Quite apart from being an insult to children, the manufacture of plastic cups and saucers for dolls houses is not a call from God (though you could of course earn a living by doing it).

Back to the line of argument in this chapter: the 'empty' world and the question how it can be filled again.

We have seen how Brunner tried to find a solution to this question. Barth was confronted with it as well. No wonder – but the difficulty is worth noticing – since both were agreed in beginning from the 'empty' world and seeing revelation as given purely in the unhistorical Word: God addresses persons, makes people persons through speaking to them.

So in this question they were agreed: how do we fill the emptiness again? In other words where do Christians get their political and social directives from? In answering this question Barth takes quite a different line from that of Brunner. Originally (I shall call this Barth 1), Barth did not go further than accepting the 'empty world' and putting it into words with an appeal to God's otherness. He tightened up the difference between God and humanity (the infinite qualitative difference) to such a degree that the traditional connecting links had to break. The world is cut off from God because God is other. This otherness meanwhile functions as a criticism, as a criticism of man and society which is radical because it is eschatological. To say that the world is empty means that the word God stands for an irremovable No to all that people (including Christians) have made clear in this world. Barth put this view forward especially in the second edition of his commentary on Romans and his 'The Christian in Society' (the so-called Tambach lecture). That produces what in theological terms is a 'between the devil and the deep blue sea' standpoint about social and political questions. Moreover in this period Barth ceased to be a member of the Christian Socialists because they associated the socialist option with God's word (which commands and redeems) and thus betrayed the position that God means a radical criticism of everything, not only to the right but also to the left. In practice we make a choice, says Barth, and from a practical point of view (but not in principle) the choice of social democracy is the best. Tillich, a friend of Barth from the 1920s, wanted to make the choice a matter of principle. In this way he again wanted it to be a matter of faith and on that point their ways parted. There must be no misunderstanding about the term 'practical' which Barth often used at this time. By it he simply meant that the political directives for action cannot be a matter of faith but must be determined by ethical and pragmatic consider-ations. In fact here Barth emerges with a doctrine of two kingdoms in the personalist elaboration of it which Troeltsch had already developed. In principle, faith provides no way of choosing between particular social and political directives. You can only infer from faith that choices of faith for particular social and political ideals are just not possible.

Later, Barth (let us call him Barth 2) brought together his doctrine of revelation in the form of christology. The 'empty world' is not empty because of our wickedness (this is the way in which you could interpret Barth 1 with a degree of goodwill) but because God has revealed himself exclusively and only in Jesus of Nazareth. The personalist basis was also broadened: it is no longer the individual person who forms the bridge between God and society but the community of persons who together make up the Christian church. This is the time of 'The Christian Community and the Civil Community', a pamphlet in which there was a theological approach to the state and politics, an approach which in general terms was similar to the personalist philosophy of the time (and of Barth himself to begin with). Hence the positive reception given to this pamphlet. Did Barth solve the problem of the 'empty world' with it? Strictly speaking not yet. God is not in the world but only in the one Word of God, Jesus Christ. However, what God plans with his sending of Jesus Christ, the 'Lordship of Christ', is confessed by the Christian church, and through the church the world (the state, politics and so on) also comes to know it. So God is only known in Christ: he is only known in the proclamation of the Word and that means that he is only present in the proclamation of the Christian church. That is not enough, even for Barth himself, since he gave the new approach that I have just described (God can only be found in Jesus Christ and therefore the world is empty) a wider scope (Barth 3). The motive for holding on to the 'empty world' remains: there is only one Word of God, Jesus Christ, and anyone who hears God mentioned outside that has encountered natural theology (and for Barth this amounts to a denial that there is only one Word of God). At the same time Barth wants to overcome the emptiness of the world. How can these two wishes be fulfilled without coming into conflict? Barth's solution is as logical as it is far-fetched. To put God outside the created world (the 'empty world') is one way of maintaining that God reveals himself only in Jesus Christ. But we can go in the opposite direction and include the created world when we talk about Jesus Christ. In that case on the one hand there is still only one Word of God, Jesus Christ, but because the created world is included in Jesus Christ concern for the creation is no longer betrayal of the one Word. Barth worked out this theological construction in his doctrine of creation: the creation (or should I say the created world or created reality?) is really already a veiled revelation of Jesus Christ, of the Word that is God with us. To read in the book of creation is to read in Jesus Christ, the one Word of God. The construction is and remains impossible. God's one Word, spoken in Jesus Christ, is the word of the reconciliation and justification of the sinner. Is creation also justification and reconciliation? But must there first be people to be justified and reconciled before God in fact justifies and reconciles? I mention just a couple of serious questions. However, Barth's concern with this construction is clear: with such an inclusive doctrine (including the creation) of God's exclusive revelation in the one Word Jesus Christ the world is no longer an 'empty' world; on the contrary, strictly speaking with this construction Barth must end up with a natural christology: all human beings know of the one Word of God, of God's salvation and commandment that has been manifested in Jesus Christ. Barth, however, did not develop his doctrine of creation in this direction but went more in the direction that we have already met in 'The Christian Community and the Civil Community'. The created world may then have Christlike features (Barth took great care to demonstrate these) but Jesus Christ is preached, believed in and confessed in the church. So only church and theology can be aware of the directives for human action. Barth carried this through into politics. At that point it was very clear how firmly he meant it. The world must be organized in an analogous way to the definitive salvation that has appeared in Jesus Christ. But do only the church and theology know of salvation in Christ? In other words, Barth's principle of analogy as a directive for action presupposes, even in politics, a knowing church over against an ignorant world. That need not have been the case, even in his own construction, had he gone further with his natural christology (leaving aside the question of whether it is acceptable). But he did not do that, and missed the theological train at a junction at which the course of a whole series of lines and branch lines part company.

Barth began (Barth 1) with radical criticism. Everything is written off, both church and world. But at the end it emerges that not everything is written off: the church and its theology give the directives. Good Barthians then say, 'Yes, but that is not the merit of the church, it is the product of grace, of the creative word of God.' Certainly, but all the water in the sea will not wash away the fact that in this way only one of the two authorities which have been written off in fact remains truly written off, namely the world (to keep to Barthian terms). That is in contradiction with things as they are, as Barth himself already has to recognize in 'The Christian Community and the Civil Community'. It is remarkable, he says there, that Rousseau already could arrive at democracy from quite different premises than those of christology. It is also in conflict with the Christian tradition, as Barth himself suspected when he again began to look for a natural theology (christology). And finally, it brings Barth into conflict with one of his most original starting points. For a whole generation – to which I myself belong – Barth was the personification of the struggle against the self-certainty and self-sufficiency of the Christian church; it has neither truth nor salvation. But in the meanwhile it has transpired that it does have these things. Through grace, certainly, and not as a possession. Yet these qualifications were also part of the substance of the opposition that the self-sufficient types of the 1930s tried to advance against Barth, and Barth rebutted that opposition perfectly. Should we not be doing the same thing today? A knowing church against an ignorant world is a construction which irrevocably makes the church once more a self-satisfied and haughty institution and the theologians who serve her those who criticize one anothers' ideologies but cannot find a place for criticism from outside – via the general human principles of humanity as criteria – because this would be to reintroduce natural theology.

I shall return to Barth, and also to many good features of his outline proclamation. Here I have been concerned with the origin of the directives for politics and social action. Barth refers politics to the church and theology. How one deals with this legacy of his we shall see in the next chapter.

11. Christology provides no directives

Strictly speaking there are few specific instructions for political and social action in Barth's theology, and according to some political theologians those that are there are more a mistake than proposals to be taken seriously. We are justified in following, for example, Dannemann in saying that Barth's theology is not political theology. That is not so surprising when we think that Barth began with an 'empty world', the other side of which lay theological personalism. Barth tried to overcome the gap through his doctrine of the one Word of God, Jesus Christ, but clearly it was not so easy to provide political and social directives from that one Word. Moreover it seems to me to be illegitimate – I mention this for the sake of completeness – to claim that his theological outline forced Barth to approve of socialism (for him, always socialism within parliamentary democracy). On the contrary, Barth was a socialist before he was Barthian. If one wants to assume dependence – which I do not really feel to be necessary – then it would be easier to make his theology arise out of his political philosophy than his political position out of his theology.

Bonhoeffer was someone whose theology, in contrast to the more personalist trend in theology, from the beginning was focussed on society (both politically and socially). That is one of the reasons why he is topical and remains so, although his theology and ethics are in themselves so clearly dated.

For a start, he sees that theological personalism is a very narrow approach to the reality of God and humanity and therefore puts the church in the foreground right at the beginning of his theological explorations: the *communio sanctorum*, which he in turn uses – also at the beginning – as a model for the world. Secondly Bonhoeffer, thoroughly a Lutheran, could never give up the classical doctrine of creation, with the result that in his works we find the doctrine of the two kingdoms cropping up again in the most unexpected places. For example we can see it in Bonhoeffer's doctrine of the mandates (about which I shall say more in a minute), which is really an attempt to put the ordinances of creation in a christological framework: wherever and whenever life is lived in accordance with the mandates – one must be a Christian to do this – the lordship of Christ is realized. The term 'lordship of Christ' already indicates an affinity between Bonhoeffer and Barth at this point. It is also in fact present when we return to the question where Christians get their political directives from. From Jesus Christ, Bonhoeffer says too. 1. The good (including what is good in political terms) is what Jesus Christ commands; 2. to know that you must be a Christian; so 3. political directives must be set up through theology (as in Barth, really through christology). But I have been careful in choosing the term 'set up'. That is something different from deriving them from theology. What Bonhoeffer did not want – even at the time when he saw Christian life being lived in a series of basic relationships which he called mandates – was that a Christian should set up another Lord alongside Jesus Christ.

What then is the difference between him and Barth if both intentions run so parallel behind the theological construction? To find an answer to that we must remember again that Bonhoeffer was a Lutheran, and certainly for Lutherans in the classical sense of this term, being a Christian coincides with being justified by faith. What or who gives a Christian a right also to commit himself or herself whole-heartedly to such basic relationship as family, society and politics? Does not this amount to submitting to the yoke of alien authorities – alien to being a Christian? The answers which Bonhoeffer gives to the question provide us with an opportunity for following his development and at the same time extending the question where Christians get their directives from. Bonhoeffer first looked for an answer which came close to the creation of an intermediate sphere between sin and grace. Not everything is either sin or grace, as a strict concentration on the doctrine of the justification of the sinner might lead us to believe, but there is also something like 'natural life' which has its own rights over against soul-snatchers and preachers of repentance and in which Christians may participate without getting a bad conscience. 'Natural' is an alien term in Reformation theology, but Bonhoeffer opts for it in order to use it to indicate that as a Christian one need not feel embarrassed about ordinary life. It does not automatically amount to serving a strange Lord.

Later Bonhoeffer gives a different answer to the same question. Certainly the most important thing ('the last thing') is and remains justification by faith. In it a person undergoes God's final judgment and to his or her amazement is acquitted. But while 'the last thing' may be the most important thing, it is not everything. It does not even make sense to talk about 'the last thing' if there is not a 'next-to-last thing', life in the associations of this world (family, social relationships, politics). For, precisely because of this next-to-last thing and what a person does or forgets to do in it, there is that judgment which ends up with the strange acquittal. Once again: ordinary life is of vital significance for Christians, though it is not the same thing as the last judgment, which decides about eternal salvation or damnation.

Bonhoeffer's last answer continues to elaborate this basic theme. In order to solve the problem he wants to remove the distinction between the last and the next-to-last reality. Ordinary life and life on the basis of belief in justification is not a double life for Christians. There is only one reality, the reality of Christ. By this Bonhoeffer means that anyone who is judged by God's justifying action in Jesus Christ does not by-pass the world, as if he or she had to use another pair of eyes in order to see human beings and society. No, in one and the same gaze he or she sees both the world (humanity and society) and the world accepted through God (in and because of Jesus Christ). Anyone who deciphers the world in this way (in politics, culture, and social questions) is not in another sphere with other lords but has moved under the lordship of Christ.

So far we have had a sketch of Bonhoeffer's development. It has been too short to show us all of Bonhoeffer, but something of him comes through. At all events we now have an answer to the basic problem that he posed to himself as a Lutheran: are Christians right to bother with society? Bonhoeffer could not solve in this christological way the next question: so what must Christians do in society? If we keep to his doctrine of the mandates, the answer to that question comes near to asserting that the content of the directives stems from creation: the mandates are the spheres of the classical ordinances of creation. What we must do there is what people have always had to do there (but failed to do). According to

Bonhoeffer, that does not change through Christian faith; what does change is that the mandates now become the sphere in which obedience is offered to Jesus Christ. The mandates become the framework for the Lordship of Christ. The difference from Barth is now clear: the directives are not derived from Jesus Christ, the Word of God (Barth), but are commanded by Jesus Christ, the one Lord (Bonhoeffer). There remains the subsequent question (which we also came up against with Barth) as to whether church and Christianity then form the bridge over which God goes to the world with God's salvation because now Jesus Christ is preached only in the church and without the preaching one does not know the implications of the lordship of Christ. Bonhoeffer's last answer to this question (which for the moment I shall pass over) is No. In contrast to Barth he ultimately accepts that the world which is not the church has come of age, and that this is a fact which the church cannot or may not again reverse. Thus the 'empty world' is now really empty; it stands on its own feet, and Christians must not try to demonstrate something of God and the gospel in it. That is a strange outcome, for what must now be the Lordship of Christ that was the starting point for everything and to which every Christian looks forward? One cannot say that the Lordship of Christ is the task of Christians and at the same time ask them to accept the fact that the world has come of age.

In his letters Bonhoeffer does envisage a solution: the 'empty world' cannot of course really be empty, but the God of the Christians is not such a manipulator of himself as the gods of this world. God is present in our world not as omnipotence but only as impotence, as someone who – as the cross of Jesus teaches us – can be forced out of it. To establish the Lordship of Jesus Christ is thus not a matter of Christians seizing power but of serving, suffering, bearing the cross – in a word, not being there for themselves but for others. And in fact, in this way it is possible to combine elements that seem to be irreconcilable: the demand that the Christian church must stop controlling humanity and society and must accept the world come of age corresponds with the requirement to establish the Lordship of Christ in this world, since this Lordship is service, suffering, and finally letting the world drive you out. But there is no indication of what and why you must serve, suffer and bear the cross. Thus Bonhoeffer's train of thought is open-ended, for each person to take further on his or her own.

How does that happen? I see that as the consequence of a theological construction which Bonhoeffer thought that he had to make – the whole of reality is Christ – and which ultimately forced him to an 'empty world'. Of course he made a virtue of necessity: 'empty' is the same thing as being able to fight its own battles and that in turn is the same thing as not regarding oneself as a Christian but following Christ in his suffering. Intrinsically that is a happy solution. Theology of the Lordship of Christ can produce domineering Christians: the Spanish Fascists had a fighter plane which bore the title Christ the King! But that is not enough. It means that the question of directives for politics and social action – the question why Christians must take suffering on to themselves – can only be answered by the situation. And as we have seen, how situations are judged depends on non-theological criteria. The actual directives for political and social action appear sufficient, despite the original intention, without theological theory.

This explains why Bonhoeffer, who in his theology, ethics and politics was markedly conservative (the opposite to what is now called left-wing), is still read and praised in Latin America, especially by Roman Catholic theologians. Bonhoeffer's message (which to many people is new) is that Christians need to be active in political and social spheres. What they must do there apart from serving the good and being ready to suffer for it, Bonhoeffer does not say. I could also say that the local Christian church must identify the good cause for which people should be willing to bear the cross. So we are back at the same point: now that other authorities (nature, creation) cannot or may not provide the political and social directives, these must be provided by theology as the outline proclamation of God's salvation in Jesus Christ ('the one Word of God'). Only: have we not come back to theology producing specific directives for action? Before we come to the conclusion that is intrinsic to the construction itself that theology (christology) cannot create directives for political and social forms of action, we must make one last attempt to saddle theology (christology) with this task; if the investigation proves to have negative results we shall of necessity be forced back to a standpoint that we have rejected: the doctrine of two kingdoms. Perhaps it provides more than we had expected and it is possible to talk about it in a way which even the theologians influenced by Barth have not thought sufficiently about.

The last attempt which I have in mind is that of political theology. That is a broad concept, of course, but as an instance of it I shall use Moltmann, and introduce others where that is useful and necessary. In order to convey Moltmann's concern as clearly as possible, I distinguish two phases in his political theology. If we are to do justice to Moltmann, we must not shut him up in his political theology – he has already landed up in a theology of creation – but because its influence on other theological outlines has been and still is great, we must subject it to an investigation.

The first phase of Moltmann's theology is really a kind of theology of history. I shall explain the meaning of this term in a moment. It is built up with the help of two starting points: (*a*) the primacy of politics and (*b*) the primacy of eschatology. In theological terminology the latter term stands for the doctrine which expresses what we must (or may) think about the coming kingdom of God, the end (eschaton).

Why the primacy of politics, and what does it mean? Moltmann had been intensively concerned with Bonhoeffer and understood his message well: politics is not an embarrassment but an activity enjoined by God as he has disclosed himself to us in Jesus Christ. But Moltmann adds another element. Whether they like it or not, theology and the church always already find themselves in an existing political field of force in which oppression and liberation regularly succeed each other. That means that whether they intend to or not, church and theology always collaborate with either the one (liberation) or the other (oppression). Political theology is theology which makes the church aware of itself; it shows that everything is politics and goes on to try to make it take the other side and thus risk its credibility. The primacy of eschatology – the second starting point – is a theological position. I can demonstrate what Moltmann means by it with a number of equations. 1. Theology is theology because it concerns itself with God's revelation. 2. Revelation, however, is revelation in Jesus Christ: there is only one Word of God. 3. Jesus Christ, God's one Word, is the Word that reveals the definitive, eschatological salvation from God. 4. Thus theology must tell us what we may and can expect from God as our coming salvation.

If we put the two starting points together we get what I have just called a kind of theology of history. We must not use this term to make any strange leaps. I use it to show that Moltmann wants to free himself from the theologians of the Word like Bultmann. For Bultmann, God is a word which points back to an experience. 'Of God we can say only what he does to us.' That is not enough for Moltmann. With Bultmann he shares the insight that the word God points to what God does: not experience, but not the personal experience of inner freedom which God gives, either. God does something in history, in the political captivity of humanity. That is what Christians have learned to believe since they heard the story of Jesus Christ, his cross and his resurrection. The God of the Exodus, who liberated the Jewish people from the slavery of Egypt, again makes himself heard in the cross and resurrection of Jesus. As the great bringer of change he breaks into our world of politics and social captivity in order to transform our history of captivity into an exodus, a history of liberation.

Is God then to be experienced in our history of disaster with his future which brings a saving action? Certainly, says Moltmann, believing eyes see him at work wherever social and political oppression are turned into liberation. Where the action is, there the God of the cross and resurrection of Jesus is at work and – we may add – there too Christians may be found on the right side of the line. This sounds enervating, and I shall not claim that Christians cannot or may not argue – in some cases have to argue – in this way. What I do claim is that Christians cannot say that something is an action of God without giving reasons for their view. Faith is not a kind of Ariadne's thread that enables you to find your way through the labyrinth of politics even with your eyes closed. The criterion may be as simple as: you need only see where liberation is fought for and you not only see God at work but you can also get to work yourself. Let me just produce one argument. How do we know whether the so-called contras in Nicaragua are concerned with the liberation of the oppressed or with seizing power? That is an important question, since in the former case as a Christian you should be positive about their struggle and in the second case negative. Now a decision is made on this cardinal question not with the eyes of faith but on good principles (the oppressed must be freed) and clear analyses (here the oppressed are or are not freed). The eyes of faith ('here I see

God reveal himself as the God of the Exodus') may well not be able to replace good principles and clear analyses; on the contrary, whether these eyes of faith have really seen God can only be demonstrated by means of these good principles and these clear analyses. Thus it is not possible to read from the historical constellation whether God is at work bringing liberation in it without having some criteria.

However, there is an even greater problem. The question was not that of the activity of God in history without further identification. That would be nothing new. Classical theology has always been aware of the action of God in history and in the world. As Creator he sustains and governs all things and directs them to the goal that he has set himself. That can be read in any catechism. But what Moltmann and most political theologians are concerned with is liberation, the saving action of God which establishes the future, the changing of the world into the kingdom of God. But can we ever say that the kingdom of God's definitive salvation is realized in history? Do our political actions of liberation really lie on the wavelength of God's eschatological action and is the kingdom of God not the kingdom *of God* precisely because it is wholly other, qualitatively different from our kingdoms, our liberation and our peace?

Moltmann has never wanted to do away with the discontinuity between our world and the world of God's definitive salvation, no matter what major problems that lands him in. What are these problems? We come upon them if we see that Moltmann increasingly develops the primacy of eschatology as the primacy of criticism and, because eschatology is concerned with God's definitive saving action, as the primacy of radical and total criticism. God is as it were only present in our history as total and radical criticism of human society. But is that still being present or is it – almost classically – being present only as the critical word of judgment?

The shift from concern for – on the one hand – God as saving presence in our old, transitory world to God as radical criticism can be demonstrated very easily by the shift from resurrection to the cross in Moltmann. By resurrection we can think, 'Look, something new is coming into our world which does not really fit it!' According to Moltmann the cross of Jesus means the same thing, but now with the stress on the negative. The cross means that God is different in this way. God cannot be involved. God is not accepted, but that happens because God is utterly different: here God's salvation does not get a foot on the ground. Moltmann's theology of the cross is theology of the radical, eschatological criticism from God of our world.

The power of this lies in the force (and the responsibility) of criticism which you can make of humanity and society in this way: if there is nothing of God's eschatological salvation in society or, to put it more strongly, if the relationship between the God of the future and today's society is only of a negative kind, the No to the existing political and social situation can be a total No.

At the same time the weakness of this emerges. The primacy of political action no sooner presents itself than it is taken up into critical negation of existing politics and society. There is nothing to be kept; instructions for the building up of society cannot be found anywhere. God only wants a complete break. Christians regard anything else as impossible for God's will.

Thus the radical eschatological criticism falls on its own sword: it condemns itself on theological grounds to inactivity. In practice an eschatological, radical and total criticism leads back – as we will recall from Barth's Tambach speech – to a doctrine of the two kingdoms, since nothing is possible without directives for the political and social order and if theology does not provide them then they must be got from general humanitarian principles: no exploitation of people and nature, no unjust distribution of goods, and so on. Moreover it is from there that Moltmann takes it into his theology of the cross. Not that there is anything against this: on the contrary, I have spent a whole book demonstrating that this is inevitable. But the original purpose was to get directives from the one Word of God, Jesus Christ, for Moltmann God's eschatological Word. That evidently does not work, however one tries. The eschatological Word is no alternative to the unhistorical Word.

Latin American liberation theology – which is also a form of political theology – is much more understandable at this point. It gets social analysis and principles which can serve as directives and criteria for criticism from the social sciences and social philosophy. In fact they must come from there. But the prejudice of a number of these theologians – which they share, for example, with Sölle and Gollwitzer – that the Marxist analysis of society uses both good

criteria and proper concepts and that one can therefore be as clear
or mistaken about the analysis of society by following the Marxists
as one can by being a Christian theologian is another matter. It is
doubtful, to say the least. Is it an analysis? Is it not rather a model
for conflict that can be applied always and everywhere, even without
analysis?

That raises yet another question: if Marx's analyses and strategy
are right, why not keep with them? Is there any reason to bring in
theology? As far as I can see, a number of the representatives of
this theology waver between two ideas: they have to use both the
Marxist analysis of society and theology. If the normative criteria
do not derive from theology, this can easily end up with something
other than theology being given a legitimizing role. If it is a question
of legitimizing the political and social activity of Christians (in other
words *that* Christians should be involved in politics), then there is
everything to be said for it. We saw how Bonhoeffer was exercised
over this point. If it is a matter of the legitimation of material,
specifically political directives, then things are different. Theology
may indeed provide legitimation, but only for what is good. I shall
come back to this later.

So no political directives emerge from the one eschatological
Word, Jesus Christ, who reveals the future. But is the Word then
perhaps an inspiration for political action? It is not that either. Our
political action cannot organize God's future. Death, tears, injustice
– all that will not disappear gradually (as the nineteenth century
wanted to believe) or through political action (as today's revolutionaries think). This does not simplify the question of what promises
the Word of the future implies for our action. To indicate the
dilemma briefly and tellingly: is the kingdom of God established
through our suffering and struggling? That is at odds with the
Christian tradition, as far as I can see. So it is not established by our
suffering and struggling. But in that case, why go on suffering and
struggling? To take the Word of the future seriously in this way –
God's future does not break through as a result of our action – does
not inspire but rather blocks our action and leads us to a paradox.
It destroys our zeal for action rather than nourishing it.

That is, unless our political action can also be significant because
it has a positive relationship to the future even if it does not illuminate
the realization of God's future. That is my own view, and I shall be

discussing it in Part IV. I shall now set out the conclusions that we can draw from the two sections of Part III.

How did Christians see the relationship between God and society with its political and social order? That was the question with which I began. It seemed to me that the doctrine of the two kingdoms, which argued in a comprehensible way that God supports (sustains) the world and gives us information about its order, must be abandoned in the light of historical investigation. Troeltsch said that there is nothing that can be called natural, and the same is true of the so-called ordinances of creation. The result was what I have called the empty world. Since then theology has worn itself out trying to fill the empty world again. But we must conclude that it has not been successful. The doctrine of the two kingdoms which was based on God's presence in creation has been done away with and we have nothing in its place: no worldly salvation which can in one way or the other be derived from God and no directives that he gives through humanity and the world. What was left was the one Word of God, preached and confessed by the Christian church, and from that one Word – Jesus Christ as the only connecting link between God and the world – we must try to derive everything, including directives for social and political action. But even if we did our best, despite assertions to the contrary, the directives which we saw – and see – being used by theology were already known and did not derive from the theology of the one Word of God, from christology or from eschatology, but from the general human principles of humanity and from a rational analysis of the situation. Moltmann's *The Crucified God* and Walter Kreck's *Grundfragen christlicher Ethik* provide sufficient evidence of that.

Why then argue so strongly that the directives must come from theology as an outline proclamation of God's eschatological salvation in Jesus Christ? We shall see that the answer is because these directives are critical, left-wing and necessarily revolutionary and traditional Christian political philosophy and ethics do not readily offer a point of contact for such directives. The 'messianic breaking down and building up' can much more easily be connected with the unhistorical Word than with creation (though in that case it is not regarded as a revelation of the future).

Now tearing down and building up may sometimes be the only task that can have Christian legitimation. But in that case this legitimation does not come with or through theology as an outline proclamation of Jesus Christ and his salvation and certainly not with or through eschatology. Political action can never be messianic action. An outline proclamation that saddles Christianity with such a task asks too much of Christians and rests on a misunderstanding of the gospel.

Bibliography

K.Barth, *Rechtfertigung und Recht*, Munich Theologische Studien 1, Basle 1938

Karl Barth, 'The Christian Community and the Civil Community' in *Against the Stream*, SCM Press 1954

R.Berki, *The History of Political Thought: A Short Introduction*, Boston 1977

D.Bonhoeffer, *Ethics*, SCM Press 1955

D.Bonhoeffer, *Letters and Papers from Prison, The Enlarged Edition*, SCM Press 1971

M.E.Brinkman, *Karl Barth's socialistische stellingname*, Baarn 1982

M.E.Brinkman, *De theologie van Karl Barth: dynamiet of dynamo voor het christelijk handeln*, Baarn 1983

E.Brunner, *Das Gebot und die Ordnungen*, Tübingen 1933

U.Duchrow, *Traditionsgeschichte und systematische Struktur der Zweireichenlehre*, Stuttgart 1970

G.Ebeling, *Word and Faith*, SCM Press and Fortress Press 1963

A.Geense, *De vrijheid van God en de bevrijding van de mens*, Nijkerk nd

L.Gilkey, *Reaping the Whirlwind. A Christian Interpretation of History*, Seabury Press, New York 1977

J.Glover, *Causing Death and Saving Lives*, Penguin Books 1977

H.Goldstein, *Befreiungstheologie als Herausforderung*, Düsseldorf 1981

F.W.Kantzenbach, *Christentum in der Gesellschaft 2*, Hamburg 1976

W.Kreck, *Grundfragen christlicher Ethik*, Munich 1975

H.M.Kuitert, 'Bonhoeffer en zijn uitleggers', *Gereformeerd Theologisch Tijdschrift* 71, 1971, 34-8

H.M.Kuitert, *Wat heet geloven?*, Baarn 1977

J.B.Metz, *Politische Theologie*, Mainz 1968

J.Moltmann, *Herrschaft Christi und Soziale Wirklichkeit nach D.Bonhoeffer*, Munich 1959

J.Moltmann, M.D.Bryant, H.W.Richardson et al., *Religion and Political Society*, Edwin Mellen Press, New York 1974

J.Moltmann, *The Crucified God*, SCM Press and Harper and Row 1974

J.Moltmann, *The Trinity and the Kingdom of God*, SCM Press and Harper and Row 1981

J.Moltmann, *Politische Theologie – politische Ethik*, Munich 1984

V.S.Naipaul, *Among the Believers*, Penguin Books 1981

W.Pannenberg, *Ethik und Ekklesiologie. Gesammelte Aufsätze*, Göttingen 1977

W.Pannenberg, *Theology and the Philosophy of Science*, Darton, Longman and Todd and Westminster Press, Philadelphia 1974

G.T.Rothuizen, *Primus Usus Legis*, Kampen 1962

V.Spulbeck, *Neomarxismus und Theologie. Gesellschaftskritik in kritischer Theorie und politischer Theologie*, Basle, Freiburg and Vienna 1977

D.Thomson, *Political Ideas*, Penguin Books 1968

IV Messianic or Christian?

12. The Sermon on the Mount in politics?

There must be politics, but messianic politics is impossible, at least as long as we think of Jesus Christ as the messiah. The previous chapter ended with this quite provocative comment. The theological standpoint from which I myself have begun so far can largely be summed up in this concentrated key sentence. The chapters in this Part will be devoted to illuminating this standpoint further and setting out the arguments for it. Now that we have seen in the previous Part what others had to say about God's concern for the world of politics and the social order, I in turn will put my own theological presuppositions on the table. I shall do this in the following way. In this chapter I shall show that messianic politics is impossible by demonstrating the impossibility of using the Sermon on the Mount in politics. But so too is the doctrine of the two kingdoms, as I shall point out in chapter 13, and go on to explain what it stands for and what it does not. In the final chapter of this Part I then draw the conclusion that politics need not be messianic to be Christian.

But first of all the Sermon on the Mount.

Many Christians today find it difficult to accept that messianic politics is impossible. Is not politics a matter of working for the ideals of peace, righteousness, freedom and sisterhood, and are these not messianic ideals? This last is certainly the case: in fact peace, justice, sisterhood and so on represent the messianic ideal of a 'whole world'. And then do we not as Christians have in the Sermon on the Mount the directives for the action we must take in order to begin to live in accordance with the messianic kingdom? That is also true, but nevertheless – as we shall see eventually, precisely because of that – the Sermon on the Mount cannot be used in politics and it makes it unavoidably clear that messianic politics is impossible. In the Sermon on the Mount Jesus gives instructions for action to Christians who want to follow him, a whole set of instructions, but the question is whether we can use these instructions for political and social action, as many Christians would want to.

To make the issue quite topical, let me illustrate the question with the problem of nuclear weapons. In our country, too, there are church associations which think that the possession and use of nuclear weapons is in conflict with God's commandment because of their devastating power and have spoken out publicly against them. Not every church organization has done that, and within the churches which did so there were many who were against such statements either because they thought that the churches should not make them or because they regarded the content of the statements as being wrong or both. There has been vigorous controversy within a number of churches which has led to polarization as a result of mass demonstrations. The controversy focussed on the possibility of positioning new cruise missiles in the Netherlands and in other parts of Western Europe, and again a number of churches, both locally and nationally, split into two groups: those for and those against. Those who were for could not understand how their fellow Christians could be so irresponsible as to throw away the trumps they held in negotiations over arms control between East and West right at the start and those who were against appealed – at least within the churches, and it is about that area that I want to talk – to the belief that all church people share with one another and the impossibility of agreeing on the possession and use of nuclear weapons. Discipleship of Jesus Christ is not war but peace, not setting up (or continuing) an arms race but ending enmity between people and groups. Being a disciple of Jesus Christ means following the instructions of the Sermon on the Mount in political and social questions as well and not carrying on a very pragmatic Realpolitik.

I shall return to the question of nuclear weapons again, though this book is not about them. At this point I need the problem they present to examine whether we can use the Sermon on the Mount in politics. Taking up the previous Part: do we not ultimately have here the directives we were looking for and do they not come from the gospel – in opposition to the conclusion that I drew there? To anticipate the result of the small investigation that I am making here: suppose that we should indeed use the Sermon on the Mount as a basis for opposition to nuclear weapons, in that case we should be opposed not only to nuclear weapons but to all modern weapons.

If it is impossible to kill in Jesus' name, or – if that is too strong – impossible to kill innocent people, then while as far as the effects of our action are concerned it makes a great deal of difference whether we kill a hundred thousand or a hundred innocent people, as far as guilt is concerned, killing a hundred innocent people is no less bad than killing a thousand: indeed killing one innocent person is an unforgivable crime. I say that only to demonstrate that 'the Sermon on the Mount' in politics means something different from making discipleship of Christ in politics dependent not on killing but on the number of dead that one does or does not find acceptable.

What does the Sermon on the Mount really say (Matt.5-7)? I am thinking in terms of just taking the text and limiting ourselves to reading it. Of course a great many good – and also nonsensical – books have been written about the Sermon on the Mount, but we need not consult them all to see how we could use it in politics. I shall begin with one of the most striking passages, Matt.5.38-48. How do we use these verses in social and political situations like those in Central America and South Africa? We can hardly say to the victims of apartheid, 'Do not resist evil but turn the other cheek.' Nor does it seem to me to be natural to call on the exploited peasants of the Central American countryside to leave the rest of their goods to their oppressors because according to the Sermon on the Mount you must go two miles with anyone who asks you to go one. Things are not like that nor can they be. We encourage the blacks of South Africa to resist, and if necessary we put rifles into the hands of exploited peasants if that is the only way in which they can protect themselves against robbery, rape and pillaging by the great landowners. We can also come closer to home: to go along with a political opponent may be in accord with the summons of the Sermon on the Mount to give someone what he asks for, to love enemies and pray for those who hate us, but things are not like this in practice nor can they be; politicans argue with one another over power and cannot exchange their watchfulness for a royal gesture that gives power to the other, since in that case they are spoiling what they are fighting for. There is more in the Sermon on the Mount than Matt.5.38-48 (and I shall return to other passages), but at this stage I can confidently say that 1. no one observes the Sermon on the Mount in politics, not even Christian politicians, whether left-wing or right-wing; 2. no one can observe the Sermon on the Mount in politics; 3. no one need observe the Sermon on the Mount while in politics.

The last statement is the hardest. I shall now defend it as well as I can and think that this is possible in a convincing way. But to do that I need 1. and 2.: no one observes the Sermon on the Mount in politics nor can anyone observe it. The texts of the Sermon on the Mount are not a summons to maintain the ideals of justice and peace and to struggle to realize the ideals. It is not only a mistake to read, for example, Matt.5.1-12 in this way, it is worse: such an appeal is to stand the passage (and the rest of Matt.5) on its head. The poor (in spirit), those who sorrow, the meek and all the others who are mentioned there up to and including those who do Christ's will are said to be blessed because the kingdom of heaven is for them or, as v.12 puts it, their reward is great in heaven. In the strongest – and to us most disconcerting – terms their reward is promised in the kingdom of heaven. That is the opposite of a call to free the poor from their oppressors and make them rich, to support the hungry with food or to rush help to those who are persecuted for the sake of the kingdom of God with an army of liberation. Those are all actions which Christians should undertake with heart and soul if necessary, but they have nothing to do with the beatitudes in Matt.5.1-12. On the contrary, the 'blessed' loses its meaning completely if the poor, the sorrowful and the persecuted are already helped, comforted and liberated here.

And then I have not mentioned that the realization of justice, freedom and peace calls for political action, the gaining of power, and that gaining power in turn often involves violence if it is to be effective: oppressors must be forcibly made to let go their grasp on power; violence must be met with violence if the poor are not to remain the eternal victims; and to remove nuclear weapons from the world conventional weapons must be increased, and so on. All these are actions which are forbidden to Christians in the other passage of the Sermon on the Mount, vv.38-48, if they want to be children of their Father who is in heaven. No one observes it since no one can observe it if he or she is serious in working for peace, freedom and justice on earth.

So it seems that the instructions of the Sermon on the Mount *cannot* be followed. In Matt.5 we are told that Christians are a peace-loving, non-violent people – and not only in Matt.5, but throughout the New Testament – but obviously Christians cannot live in this way. However, at this stage that would be too hasty a conclusion to draw. To obey the Sermon on the Mount is possible, may well be possible, but in that case it presupposes a Christian church which has no more to expect of this world and in turn does not expect any more from it. Moreover in Matt.5 it is called on to put its hope in the kingdom of heaven, and meanwhile to shine as a light in the darkness, being different from others to the point of renouncing self-defence, becoming a community of martyrs, the drop-outs of this world, and being a group of disciples of Jesus in this way leaving the world to itself rather than manipulating it. To go the way of the cross, what Bonhoeffer called the way of helplessness, to be sheep in the midst of wolves: what is there against living as the church in this way? Nothing. Except having the courage to be a drop-out and to suffer for a conviction, having unshaken trust in the reward that is great in the kingdom of heaven and an inspiring relationship of faith with Jesus. To keep to practical matters: why should not groups or individuals today refuse to do military service on the basis of their faith or stop paying taxes or opt out of the health service? There is nothing against that in the Sermon on the Mount: on the contrary, the Sermon on the Mount tells us precisely what a Christian church must do in such a situation if it is to be the Christian church. Groups and individuals have also tried often in the course of history – though not in a situation which gave occasion for it – to present themselves as drop-outs and thus to show that they have settled their hopes on the other world of the kingdom.

Of course these attempts indicate that romantic ideals also played a part: the Christian church as a wholly other society which prefers to allow itself to be swept away by the world rather than to enter into a compromise. But that does not disqualify an ideal of life like the Sermon on the Mount. Anyone who wants to live in that way perhaps does not always need to, but always deserves our respect and admiration.

Of course we must be aware that a church of lambs among the wolves cannot at the same time be a church which seeks to attain political power, the power of lambs, so to speak. You cannot have it both ways: renouncing power and becoming a lamb and then trying to gain power as a lamb. At least you cannot do that without betraying the way of the cross and thus removing it again as a way.

It seems to me to be one of the temptations in the wilderness which Jesus himself faced, according to the same Gospel of Matthew. Political power ('I will give you all the kingdoms of the world') or the way of the cross: which is the way of the Messiah?

And yet – to return to the thread of the argument – most Christians do not opt for a life according to the Sermon on the Mount. Even mutual relations within the church community – for which the instructions in the Sermon on the Mount are clearly meant – seem to take little heed of the Sermon on the Mount. Are there reasons, perhaps even good reasons, for this? Not when it comes to mutual relationships within the Christian church. There power, prestige and prosperity need not play any part, and if they do, that goes against the life-style of the church. Thus it finds itself on a fatal course. However, we are not investigating the significance of the Sermon on the Mount for dealings between Christians, but for politics. I have already demonstrated why Christians cannot follow the Sermon on the Mount there. I shall now argue that Christians must not do so either ('must' here used in the sense of 'need').

1. I have described politics as the cherishing of social and political ideals and the gaining (or maintaining) of power to realize them. Politics cannot happen without what in one of the most salient passages of the Sermon on the Mount is denied to Christians: prestige, power, compulsion and if necessary violence. But does that mean that politics is condemned or – especially as happened under Dopersen – forbidden to Christians? I shall go on to give another answer to this (under 2). Let me say here that the use of prestige, power, compulsion and force is necessary for the realization of political ideals, but that does not yet indicate that any political ideal is a good one nor does it mean that prestige, power, compulsion and force may be exercised without criteria. From Augustine on, classical Christian ethics already recognized the just war, a term by which people meant that if war has to be waged, then it must be subject to certain rules.

So the power-struggle is necessary for politics. If Christians want to exert influence in seeking to realize political and social ideals (or if they want to help to oppose their realization) then – against the instructions of the Sermon on the Mount – they must take part in the struggle for power, though that implies that norms may and must be applied to the struggle. Influence for what? That brings me to a second point, which is at the same time a second answer to the question whether politics is forbidden ground for Christians.

2. Can Christians not renounce a concern to exert influence? That sounds humble and in accord with the Sermon on the Mount, but it is impossible, or rather, Christians cannot want to do that. People and society are of such a nature that anyone who consistently renounces influence, power and even violence hands society over to the men of violence. At this point two convictions converge. The first is the Christian doctrine of sin, which is by no means the worn-out carpet that many people have made of it but rather an extremely contemporary piece of experiential wisdom in the Christian church: people are not as nice as we would like, especially where prestige, power or material interests are involved, i.e. in political and social questions. The book that Reinhold Niebuhr wrote about politics and the social order was called *Moral Man and Immoral Society*. It brings up the puzzling situation that on his or her own a person is usually very concerned for fellow human beings, but this ceases to happen when people form political and social groups. And yet the same people are involved. The Christian doctrine of sin gives a sober and not very optimistic view of the world and society. Anyone who forgets it becomes an idealist who is incapable of political action. The second conviction that Christians cannot let go of is that the idea of a real society has to be made concrete even in a world which is not ideal (Niebuhr's immoral society). Turning the other cheek is not a good way of doing this. On the contrary, there is no reason whatsoever why one should not hit back at someone who is violent. Or without the imagery: in a chaotic world the renunciation of power and even violence never succeeds in delivering the weak from the strong. If there is a concern to realize in our world a society which is just to a greater or lesser degree, then the Sermon on the Mount cannot help us and we must use violence in order to protect the weak.

3. The renunciation of violence, turning the other cheek and giving away one's cloak could be elevated as a political ideal if the whole world were a church in the sense of following the instructions of Jesus Christ, including those in the Sermon on the Mount. In that case we would find ourselves in a theocracy in which – as we have seen – church and people coincide. But that is not the actual situation and certainly was not presupposed in the Gospel in which the

Sermon on the Mount was handed down. There – though this applies
to the whole of the New Testament, as the origin of the Christian
tradition – church and society do not overlap but the church is a new
start, another beginning, a citizenship of a very different state, as
Augustine put it so vividly, in the midst of earthly states. For this
church the instructions of the Sermon on the Mount are significant,
but not for politics. To make a political programme of this is to
forget that belonging to this church (being a citizen of the kingdom
of heaven) is presupposed by the Sermon on the Mount and that
according to Matthew outside this church there are no conditions
for belonging to it and being obedient to it.

Moreover, Christians who want to make the Sermon on the
Mount a political programme find that they are contradicting
themselves in more than one way. As we saw, politics is not just
maintaining ideals of peace and justice – messianic ideals – but also
gaining power to realize the ideals. Now to establish the kingdom
of the messiah with the help of political power (or even with violence)
is to fight for the new order with the weapons of the old. That means
more of the same thing: more power struggle, more prestige, more
wars of self-interest and nothing different, nothing new.

But obedience to the messiah and his kingdom cannot be achieved
by means of power. At this point the waggon goes off the rails. The
Sermon on the Mount not only requires Christians *not* to take part
in the struggle for power, but what it *does* require of them, obedience
to the commandment of Christ, can only be regarded as very
optional. The use of the means of power (for example political
action or the formation of parties) turns this obedience into its
opposite and compromises the way that the messiah himself has
taken. The messiah gained followers not through power or violence
but through the voluntary acceptance of his gospel and command.
I could also say that it is not by making the Sermon on the Mount a
political programme but by making it the content of the proclamation
of Christ that the Christian church finds a way for the messiah and
his kingdom to enter into this world.

That also answers the question whether in that case we must not
interpret the Sermon on the Mount in eschatological terms in order
to cope with it, i.e. in the sense that the situation as described here
will one day become reality. That is indeed possible – in fact necessary – if we mark off the first twelve verses of Matt.5, the Beatitudes.

Indeed one day those who weep shall be comforted, the meek shall inherit the earth and the persecuted shall receive their reward in heaven. That is the obvious meaning of these verses, and their intention is that these people, living in a situation which is the exact opposite, shall be encouraged to tolerate things for the moment.

But we cannot extend this interpretation to read: one day it will come about that all people shall leave their gifts before the altar and then be reconciled with their brothers. Or, a time will come when all people will turn the other cheek if they have first had a blow on the right cheek. In the eschaton there will no longer be disputes between people or blows or differences. The Sermon on the Mount presupposes a situation in which such things are the order of the day. It comprises instructions for the life of the Christian community in a situation which is not blessed with eschatological salvation. In the eschaton the Sermon on the Mount – thank God – will have become meaningless.

So this is not messianic politics: the kingdom of God is clearly not preached by Jesus as a political ideal that his successors in this world have to realize. In this world they will simply suffer oppression. The kingdom of God is another world into which people will (or will not) enter, but in that case they must prepare for it now. In the gospel that is called repentance. So the message with which Jesus begins his ministry is, 'Repent and believe in the gospel' (Mark 1.15). Jesus thus makes the way in which people live eschatologically important: participation in the coming kingdom of God depends on it. Giving the hungry something to eat, the thirsty something to drink, housing strangers, clothing the naked, visiting the sick and those in prison – these are all things which people do not rate highly; according to Jesus what matters is whether or not you become a member of the other world, the kingdom of God depends on them (Matt.15.31 etc.).

How the other world looks from God's side is not described in so many words, but a good deal is suggested in all kinds of images from Jesus' actions and life-style: the sick are healed, the lame walk, the dead are raised, the dumb speak and the hungry are fed. That is symbolic language for what the Jewish community of Jesus' day imagined as a whole world, a messianic world, the world of the kingdom of God, terms which here we can use interchangeably: they denote the same thing. In terms of this symbolic language Jesus proclaims the other world of God. We have no other words for it than those of the messianic dream, the dream of the world as it really should be, or rather, the world from which what we experience as disaster has vanished.

But that stresses only that the other world of God is not a political ideal and that he commissions us to realize it. The symbolic language may make that clear to us. It is such that we must say: that does not happen here, we cannot remove sickness, injustice and sin from the world nor bring the dead to life again. But Jesus' instructions in the Sermon on the Mount make it quite clear: politics cannot be carried on without power and violence, but the other world of God is precisely the world from which power and violence have disappeared.

In order to avoid any misunderstanding, all this does not mean that Jesus may not also be a political guru. Just as the bourgeois theologians of the last century found in him the teacher of humanity, so the liberation movements of today can find in him all that they need, above all if we again think of the symbolic language in which he proclaimed the kingdom of God. If it is good politics, politics is simply trying to realize those things which together indicate features of the messianic world: the changing of unjust situations, the making or keeping of peace, the quest for sisterhood, and so on. That we can only put right a very little bit of all this and that we use the wrong means to do so does not alter this fact.

But Jesus did not present himself as the great helmsman of a political movement which would change our world into a whole world. He is not the moral teacher nor even the political activist. He is more. The apostle Paul was not wrong when he made Jesus the Christ: he was that already. We do not contribute to the messianic kingdom. The teaching in the Sermon on the Mount makes that quite clear. From it we learn something that I have presupposed all the time: it is not achieved through politics, since with politics we are stuck with the old means (compulsion and force). Nor do we get anywhere by ignoring politics, since in that case we would only become the drop-outs of the world in the way which the Sermon on the Mount describes. If the kingdom of God does not come about through 'doing' or 'not doing', there is only one conclusion left: it is different, totally different. We do not know what it is, we only know that it is eternal salvation from God and that the one who preached it asked us to believe in him and repent, so that we could enter the kingdom of his own.

I shall return to these matters – and their implications. This chapter has served to demonstrate that we cannot use the Sermon on the Mount in politics and that there are good reasons why we cannot. Jesus did not preach the kingdom of God as a political ideal, although he spoke about it in terms with which people down the centuries have associated their political ideals, but as the other world of God which we can muse on only in dreams. In eschatological faith we sum up all that is impossible here and which must nevertheless concern us if we want a whole world.

Finally, refraining from using the Sermon on the Mount for politics does not mean that we introduce faith into politics. Nor does it mean dismissing the Sermon on the Mount. So perhaps not everything is politics? That implies that a Christian is a citizen of two kingdoms, or at least he or she is according to classical theology. But that already brings me to the next chapter.

13. The doctrine of the two kingdoms

Classical theology has never accepted the Sermon on the Mount in politics. If we remove the negative connotations from the word, it is a form of modernism. A number of modern Christians want to keep faith and politics together. For them faith is the Sermon on the Mount. Anyone who takes the Sermon on the Mount out of politics takes faith out of politics: that is the argument.

In this Part I shall claim that the argument rests on a short circuit. That was already indicated in the previous chapters, but here I shall argue in so many words that faith and politics does not mean gospel and politics (and therefore also does not mean the Sermon on the Mount and politics) while conversely politics without the Sermon on the Mount may be politics which does not take its directives from the gospel but is not necessarily for that reason politics without faith.

There is more than one reason why that may sound strange. Partly it is a question of terminology, and that already blurs questions. For example, what does the word gospel mean? I shall use it here in the limited meaning of a saving message of reconciliation with God through Jesus Christ, but one can also understand it to denote justice and peace as a message of salvation. In that case, of course, the gospel has everything to do with politics and the Dutch Communist Party has just as evangelical politics as, let us say, the Evangelical People's Party. I do not use that terminology, and in the course of this chapter it will become clear why I do not. It seems to me to be a way of speaking which not only disguises what the Christian church is about and therefore puts it at risk but also contributes (has contributed) to letting Christian faith go up in the smoke of a social and political moralism. The word faith, too, has more than one meaning. But the next chapter will be about that.

There is more behind this than being bewitched by language. We are unaccustomed to reckoning with two ways in which we experience God's dealings with humanity and the world: on the one hand through the word of reconcilation, the preaching of Christ, and on the other through the world in which we live, e.g. both in the church and in the suburbs of a major city. The reason for this lack of familiarity has to do on the one hand with a one-sided personalist accent on the theology of the Word, especially on the way in which Barth reduced the duality to a unity (the one Word Jesus Christ). On the other hand this outline proclamation would not have got so established were we not confused over the experience of God in ordinary life. Where do we meet him today, in what things or events? Sunday 10 of the Heidelberg Catechism begins a section there, but for many people these are obsolete ideas of faith.

On these matters: in this chapter I shall examine the view that God encounters us not only in the Word of reconciliation, Jesus Christ, but also in everyday life. I shall do that under the heading of the doctrine of the two kingdoms, a theme that I have already touched on but now will examine specifically. The doctrine of the two kingdoms has many forms and many themes are combined in it. There is good reason for the existence of a study which is called *Im Irrgarten der Zwei Reichen* ('In the maze of the doctrine of the two kingdoms'). In fact the doctrine is something of a labyrinth, but we keep coming up against it, and there must be a reason why it returns generation after generation. A very simple but extremely fundamental reason, as we shall soon see. For the theme with which we are concerned, faith and politics, it is also of fundamental significance and has remained so.

The doctrine of the two kingdoms is a solution, but a different one, for the problem with which contextual theology saw itself confronted: how can we give theological expression to the fact that we are concerned not only with Jesus Christ but with the context (black – white/freedom – oppression/man – woman and similar social and political questions)? Contextual theology tries to get this context within the outline proclamation of the Christian message of salvation, Jesus Christ, and in this way to explain why Christians 'act in context': being concerned with the context is really being concerned with Jesus. He is already in it; people experience him there as liberator from social and political misery, with all the problems that this construction provokes. Is Jesus above all a command (to attack the context and change it) and is his salvation political and social by nature? Is that salvation? I have already indicated a number of these problems in the Part dealing with contextual theology, and we shall encounter others here. The doctrine of the two kingdoms says that they are not necessary (and of course itself creates yet other problems); the context within which the Christian message of salvation is proclaimed, the world of women, men, black, yellow, white, philosophers, laity and so on is not Jesus Christ, does not need to be changed to become Jesus Christ and therefore is not an element of the Christian outline proclamation either. Nevertheless Christians are concerned with it, they even experience God in it (and in a much more daring way than contextual theology ventures), but in that case they experience God who as creator is occupied with his world, a way of being occupied which is different from his reconciling and pacifying action and is not done away with by this last. That is the way in which the context is put into words as experience and task in the doctrine of the two kingdoms.

The term 'doctrine of the two kingdoms' is misleading, and is too suggestive of two areas. But because it has become established I am keeping to it. Moreover, it is wrong to speak of *the* doctrine of the two kingdoms. One cannot do this any more than one can talk of *the* church. There are many churches, and so there are also many forms of the doctrine of the two kingdoms. But they all go back to one and the same basic problem and therefore they can all be summarized under the heading of two kingdoms.

Now what is the simple and at the same time fundamental datum which, as far as I can see, must irrevocably lead to a form of the doctrine of the two kingdoms? It is the perennial problem that was created with the coming of the Christian church and will therefore remain as long as there is a Christian church: the Christian church preaches another kingdom, the kingdom of the definitive eternal salvation from God, and interprets itself as the first earnest of that salvation in the midst of a world of disaster. I deliberately said 'interprets itself as the first earnest'. Only in this way can we see that the 'eternal problem' of duality appears wherever Christians do not run away from their own confession. This confession is not just 'Behold I make all things new'. It also contains faith in the coming kingdom of God. No hope and courage would be left if as the Christian church we could not spell it out letter by letter. But the construction of Christian doctrine would be violently disrupted, The doctrine of the two kingdoms would be no longer a problem since there would be no duality at all, if the Christian church were to forget that the kingdom is already present and that the Christian church is the community of people who experience the salvation of that kingdom. Anyone who is in Christ is a new creation. This leads to the duality which lies at the roots of the doctrine of the two kingdoms and thus it is clear at the same time that a doctrine of the two kingdoms can only be avoided by explaining the whole world as a new creation (in a hidden way) or reducing the new creation to a mere accompaniment. Neither of these two options represents the Christian tradition. At the end of this section I shall show why not.

The eternal salvation of God for humanity and the world which can no longer be devoured by death or time is, according to Christianity, a new element in the world as we know it, an invasion from another dimension. In a variety of expressions we see this confession returning in the history of the Christian church: eternity enters time, the supernatural grace of God appears in the natural world, the other side can be experienced in this side, God's future enters the present, the kingdom of grace comes up against the kingdom of sin, and so on. I am not leaving them out of my account, but introduce them only to stress the aspect of the other, the new, which according to the Christian church is given with the appearance of Jesus Christ in our world and which as far as content is concerned presents itself as a definitive redemption, eschatological salvation, the eternal peace of God with man – again, here we have a multiplicity of words and ideas which Christian tradition has used in the course of history. To know what we are concerned with – under what terms I shall discuss later – I shall from now on speak of eternal salvation, or salvation for short, as the content of the gospel of Jesus and thus, in conformity with Christian tradition, of the forgiveness of sins, peace with God, the new life and eternal security. Salvation defines itself as salvation in contrast to damnation: sin, death and helplessness as characteristics of being human as we know it. To make the point again, the outstanding feature of Christianity is that it gives an answer to these characteristics of lostness which are attached to being human. The proclamation is that salvation came into our world of disaster through Jesus Christ (his words and works) and that the church is a community of people who believe in that salvation and know it in their lives: 'Anyone who is in Christ is a new creation'.

But this same Christian church which opens up a way into the eternal salvation of God with its preaching of the gospel cannot but recognize that there was (or is) something like salvation before it issued a summons to faith and conversion with its proclamation. The world is not purely the kingdom of the devil. This argument has also been used, and constantly plays a role, both in Augustine and in Luther. But the experience was otherwise: the world is not just the kingdom of the devil. Death, sin, catastrophes in nature, oppression by the powerful are not the only reality. There is also happiness; people have children and are happy, they make a society in which life can go on, and even if the society does not have a just structure they can still be happy in it, love and be loved, and be happier to be alive than dead. I deliberately mention a number of obvious experiences which go to make up life, natural life according to Bonhoeffer: no sin and no grace, yet something good to share, salvation. Not eternal salvation, but salvation as well-being, which is what I shall call this experience. How can salvation as well-being exist while at the same time the background of the message of the gospel is damnation and the lostness of man and the world? Classical theology derived the experience of well-being from God as creator and preserver of his creatures. The disruptive effect of sin was not recognized, but God was thought to keep humanity and the world from total chaos. So there was much to experience which was true, good and beautiful. All that was to be seen as a relic of the good creation, preserved thanks to God's sustaining grace.

We would put things differently today, as we would many theological constructions from the past. It is especially impossible for us to achieve the historical conception of things as being in 'remnants'. We cannot point to a time when everything was still good, a time which subsequently was replaced by a period which began with the fall. So nothing has been left of the ordinances of creation. We cannot even use the idea of ordinances of preservation, much loved by German Lutherans (even Bonhoeffer praised them for a while). The history of the development of our world took a completely different course, as far as we can see. But the basic experience from which the notion of 'remnants' proceeds is as indisputable as ever; there is salvation as well-being, the salvation of creation, salvation within the world or whatever else it may be called; it also exists where the salvation of the gospel is not recognized or believed in and it is to be derived from God who as creator and preserver does not leave humanity and the world in the lurch.

Here the duality which the doctrine of the two kingdoms tries to sort out is presented to us in all its uncontradictability. We need not be further occupied with the misuse that has been made of this doctrine. We are not concerned with the history of the doctrine of the two kingdoms. Moreover, there is hardly an item of doctrine which has not been open to misuse when it comes to gaining power over others or getting and keeping privileges. But surely we do not do away with the doctrine of sin because it can so easily lead to political and social quietism? I mention only one of the many items of doctrine which could be a candidate for elimination, if misuse were the criterion for abolition. We must not be as stupid as that, even over the doctrine of the two kingdoms. Nor must we make a caricature of it through stubbornness or unwillingness. The duality is not that of realists and idealists, scientific thought and faith, autonomy and acceptance of norms, secular and Christian, without God and with God, and similar combinations, but the duality of God, who deals with his world as creator and preserver and also as reconciler and redeemer. The duality is a Christian experience; only Christians know it, since they introduced it themselves with their proclamation of another kingdom. Therefore the doctrine of the two kingdoms raises problems only for Christians. The one kingdom is not the other; only Christians, therefore, can enter the fog. The one kingdom cannot be played off against the other: only Christians can give way to the temptation to do that. The same goes for conflating the two kingdoms. I shall devote the rest of this chapter to these three pitfalls. And the other side is the reward that awaits if we avoid these pitfalls.

The one kingdom is not the other. If we confuse salvation as well-being with eternal salvation, we make political or social salvation the content of the Christian proclamation. But from a Christian point of view that is impossible. Anyone who is in Christ is a new creation – not anyone who lives in a democratic, revolutionary or whatever other kind of political order. Unless we can keep the political context for Jesus Christ himself (which is impossible): but is anyone a new creation, a new person because he or she is in a new political order? Political structures must be renewed, but so too must the people whose relationships are regulated by them. Otherwise we have not got far. Political order cannot make a new creation, but it can further the salvation of creation or break it off. Therefore the political order is an extremely important matter and it is with good reason that classical theology devoted a section in the context of the doctrine of the two kingdoms to the authorities, as one of the instruments with the help of which God as creator and preserver wards off chaos, turns away injustice and protects the weak against the strong.

We can see that the one kingdom is not the other from more than the fact that well-being is still not salvation. To confuse the two kingdoms brings our own action into play, since in the one kingdom it has quite a different role from that in the other. Not to see the difference in place and function has catastrophic consequences for the Christian confession. As the Christian proclamation has it, eternal salvation is a gift from God, a gift which people receive freely. No one brings about his or her eternal security and peace with God through keeping to the rules of any game. It is not a product of human action, individual or collective. But well-being, as the salvation of creation, is a different matter. We have to do something about that; even more, we are responsible for it within the limits of the possible. At this point again there seems to be at least some sense that the duality of the doctrine of the two kingdoms is indispensable for keeping the ship of the church afloat: anyone concerned with eternal salvation (the forgiveness of sins and peace with God) who acts as though he or she were concerned with political salvation (i.e. well-being) confuses the two kingdoms by making the gospel law – to use classical terms. And of course vice versa: anyone who does not make social and political salvation a personal concern does the same thing.

By contrast, taking into account the difference leads us out of many impasses in which we are landed by all kinds of theological projects of today. It can help us to explain much which otherwise remains inexplicable – or needs such complicated explanations that what has to be explained gets completely lost – and that has a liberating effect. It explains how it comes about that there is salvation outside the Christian church; not eternal salvation but the salvation of creation. It explains why there is good everywhere: loving and being loved, the natural life and the forgiveness of sins. The one is not the other and the two cannot be derived from each other but go together. It also explains why Bible and church are not needed to show people the knowledge of good and evil. On the contrary, the Bible – to keep to that – presupposes that this knowledge is already present. When God himself calls on Israel not to choose anyone but him as their God, he appeals to their knowledge of moral virtues. He is faithful, will not leave them in the lurch, and so on; this can only mean that Israel already knew the moral virtues of fidelity and loyalty before God commended himself to them by means of these virtues. Thus the Bible itself shows that there was moral knowledge before there could be any mention of a Bible. Classical theology derived this knowledge – humanitarian principles – from God himself, who as creator did not leave himself without witness but gave information about himself and did good.

This also makes it clear what subject matter we are dealing with in connection with the doctrine of the two kingdoms. I shall sum up the most important points.

1. We have been able to establish in the previous chapters that the principles for political and social action cannot be derived from the gospel, 'the one Word of God'. We now see that they need not be. Basic humanitarian principles were already there before ever the gospel was proclaimed; they were also there before Jesus went through Judaea with his preaching. In so far as Jesus is seen as the guru for politics – there is nothing against that – he does not say new things but what was already known. On questions of morality, he does not want anything different but more of the same thing: love not just for friends but also for enemies; giving not only to those from whom you expect something back but also to those who have nothing to give in return, and so on.

2. That these principles for good action come from creation, are known by all and are not the fruit of 'the one Word of God' makes them no less important for Christians to observe. Jesus made use of them; therefore a good deal of liberation theology can refer to the historical person of Jesus over a good many things. In that case it is appealing to what Jesus established: the wisdom and knowledge that stems from creation. Moreover Christians must also have these principles – humanity – in so far as they are also the norms by which they are treated by others. And finally, what is wrong with faith in

creation? Christian theology can hardly have removed sin and the grace of creation from below.

3. One need not be a Christian to know what good action is. Augustine, and after him Luther, sought to see the difference between Christians and non-Christians not in knowing but in doing. But even that is too much of a good thing. The world is also involved, says Abraham Kuyper. We forgive him the pedantry of the comment, since he went on to say that the church was involved, too. However, if the humanitarian principles are common property, there can be collaboration between Christians and non-Christians, wherever and whenever it is a matter of specific political and social aims which withstand the test of criteria for humanity.

4. There is also salvation outside the church, the salvation of creation, or even well-being. So not all directives need derive from the gospel nor need everything be regulated by the church in order to be healthy for people. On the contrary, there is no reason why churches should be better equipped to see to the well-being of a society than the society itself. Referring to Part I, I could add that theology need not be social criticism or a theory of political action. It can be, as we saw, but there is no reason why it should be: political and social salvation is the salvation of creation, well-being, and how people can achieve that is not for theology to say. Others can do it better. Let theology explain salvation to us, definitive salvation and the way to it: peace with God, reconciliation and life as a new creation.

Instead of confusing one kingdom with the other we can also play one off against the other. The duality, very easily ending up in division, has a double focus in which the one perspective becomes the rival of the other: you live for the 'last thing' or the 'next-to-last' thing, you are faithful to earth or heaven, it is a matter of well-being or salvation, the one kingdom or the other – the question can come up in many forms of words and lead to confusion. But the question is wrong. Each kingdom has an indissoluble value of its own. The doctrine of the two kingdoms is concerned with the two ways in which God is occupied with man and the world. The two ways are not interchangeable: creation is not reconciliation and redemption and vice versa. Nor can they be played off one against the other: God's creation cannot be detached from his reconciling and redeeming action and vice versa. So you cannot say that the world is about the church, as Augustine (and Karl Barth) thought; nor can you say that the church is about the world (Schleiermacher, Ritschl). These are solutions which 'remove' the problem.

Nor can the two kingdoms be combined. It would be an attractive solution if we could replace 'above' and 'below' with 'now' and 'soon'. In earlier books I myself have moved in this direction, but how far can we go with it? Apparently it represents a step in the direction of overcoming the duality in so far as there is a connection between 'now' and 'soon': what we do now has a significance for 'soon' or, put differently, 'soon' is the fruit of all that went before. But from the perspective of the Christian tradition that is an impossible way of looking at things. There is no line which runs from 'now' to 'soon', at least if we write 'Soon' with a capital letter and mean by it the kingdom of God. With our political action – if it turns out well – we achieve well-being in some respects for some people in some places at some times. But we do not achieve salvation, forgiveness of sins, eternal life. Dying cannot be reversed by any political or social action. Any attempt to combine the two kingdoms comes up against this fact. Eternal salvation never comes from salvation (well-being) within the world. A Christianity which surrendered itself to that would land up in the same belief in progress as nineteenth-century liberal theology (Ritschl) which saw the kingdom of God on the horizon as the flickering perspective of the moral effort of the whole of humanity, with the difference that the moralism of that time had a bourgeois stamp and that now politics has a left-wing colouring. A large number of arguments can be advanced against such a belief in progress – and therefore politics. I have already mentioned the moralism which is connected with it. But the irrefutable argument against it is and remains death: there is no political or social solution for that.

That is the outcome of the doctrine of the two kingdoms: there is no such thing as messianic politics and therefore it cannot look for a place in the outline proclamation of the Christian church. Is that disappointing? Anyone who thinks so is under a misapprehension about the way to and from the kingdom of God. He or she is under a misapprehension about the outline proclamation. The messianic dream of 'the whole world of God' does have a place in it, but not in the way in which a number of political theologians have supposed. The messianic dream is indeed a Christian dream, but it was not invented by Christian faith nor is it a possession of the Christian church. The dream can also be bought in other shops. That has to be said first. There have been messianic dreams in all kinds of cultures, and some have looked backwards as well as forwards: backwards to the former golden age, the unspoilt creation, or forwards to the untouched future. Christianity knows both longings at the same time: the good creation at the beginning and the messianic future at the end. It shares the messianic longing with many other societies. As a 'warm gulf stream' (Bloch) it goes through the history of culture, settling wherever it can find a place. Jesus too preached the 'whole world'. As I have already remarked, he confirmed the wisdom that comes from creation and this includes utopian longings. But that is not the whole Jesus, nor is the proclamation of messianic ideals of peace and justice the only thing that the gospel stories tell us he did. Christianity understood that well. The longing for the 'whole world' does not disappear; it makes utopia a promise of God. That is how it appears in the Christian proclamation. But at the same time Christianity knows the snag, the failure of history, disaster. More is needed to reach the kingdom of God than going in that direction. The obstacles are not what we supposed: they lie in human beings themselves. This is where many messianic movements, whether secular or religious, are naive: they are children's crusades to the promised land. So while the messianic dream of the 'whole world' indeed stands in the proclamation, it does not do so as a political ideal to which people can dedicate themselves. According to Christian faith the realization of the kingdom of God takes another course. Christianity connects its realization with redemption, peace with God and the conquest of death and the fear of death through Jesus Christ, so the way into the kingdom is personal: a person enters it through faith and repentance and becomes a new creation.

No one can believe for someone else nor repent in his or her place. So there is not a collective way to the kingdom of God any more than a people is affected collectively by the divine judgment. That is the case in politics. The decisions of the majority – or in a junta, of individuals – bring the collective, the whole people, salvation or disaster. But even then it would be a great mistake to distill from that the idea that people exist only as a collective and are not personally responsible: and more than a mistake to ordain that they *may* exist only as a collective. That can only be the crafty theory of a dictatorial regime, which is not open to contradiction by personal conscience.

So we have discussed politics and salvation within the world. What majority or what junta can collectively realize the salvation of the kingdom of God or save us from having to go on existing personally and choose whom we shall serve, God or mammon? In Christian terms that is an impossible view of things, and as far as I can see a consequence of the far-reaching identification with the response of faith with thinking in political terms. The salvation of the kingdom of God is not collective like political salvation, and participation in it is not a collective event but happens by the changing of a person: he or she must become a new person, a new creation. Here the kingdom of God finds a beginning. So the 'advance guard of life' (Gollwitzer) is not the people as a whole, but within the people the church, however offensive we may sometimes find that. And what makes the church the advance party is not primarily its progressive character in solving social and political questions. It is involved if church people are also an advance party in this respect but there is no need for such an advance party to be made up of Christians. Non-Christians also know the way to indicate in politics very well. The Christian church is the advance party of life through the forgiveness of sins and living by the Spirit. The Spirit brings freedom, including freedom for political and social action for others. In this sense Christians may be asked about their political interests and zeal. But that is not what makes them the advance party.

Is that dissuasive language? Certainly. In so far as political and social actions – which are always collective undertakings and directed by collective regulations – do not take on messianic character in this way I am dissuading Christians from political manipulation. But non-messianic is something different from non-Christian, as we shall see.

14. Faith, politics and ethics

The claim that politics is not in fact messianic (no one observes the Sermon on the Mount), cannot be messianic (politics goes wrong if it uses the Sermon on the Mount) and need not be messianic (the doctrine of the two kingdoms is not) in order to be called Christian, needs a practical conclusion: what does that mean? That is what I shall consider in this chapter. In my argument 'Christian' amounts to 'in terms of Christian faith'. So what I shall do is make a link between faith and politics in a way which – contrary to my demonstration in previous Parts – can withstand the test of a theological criticism. If politics cannot be messianic, what then?

I am devoting a whole chapter to this so that mistakes in the construction of this combination can be eliminated: they would deprive the church and faith of their natures and lead to the diminution of political concern. A mistake in construction can lead to disaster: in the next Part I shall have more to say about that than I did in the previous one. In order to explore adequately the question what faith has to do with political action we shall deal with it in two stages: 1. do people who believe need to be involved in political action because of their faith? and 2. one stage further, do they need politics for their faith? By faith I mean faith in God as he is presented to us through Jesus Christ. Later in this chapter I shall introduce a distinction into the term faith.

The answer to the first question begins with the removal of a misunderstanding. It is not the case that we have only recently understood that politics is important and is therefore a must for Christians, whereas previous generations did not realize this. Granted, originally primitive Christianity had no political commitment, or rather, political involvement was not its characteristic. Of course from the beginning it was a political factor, not only through being a religious community but also – in a more direct sense – through its teaching. But from this last perspective too the most we can say is that Christianity was only involved in politics indirectly. Some Christians – including theologians – regard that as an ideal: the Christian church is simply there, and the more that it is itself, for example the more clearly it preaches the justification of the sinner or celebrates the eucharist, the more significant it will prove as a political factor. The church does politics not through doing politics but through being the church. This is, for example, the argument put forward by Karl Barth in his book *Justification and Justice*. It is not a wrong standpoint but it is not very satisfying. In the first place, we cannot regard the starting point of Christianity as the ideal situation. Even though it may be there in the Bible it remains a historically determined position which may perhaps give us a direction but which we cannot regard as a norm or criterion. Yesterday is never a criterion for today without further stipulations. Secondly, in this case yesterday certainly cannot be a criterion since politics is carried on in a completely different way from that in the time of earlier Christianity: far more people are involved in it and their influence on what happens is much greater. That in turn means that political action has become more important in the course of history.

That has also been seen by the Christian church. It is not that our grandparents did not engage in politics because they regarded faith far too much as a private matter. The so-called privatization of faith – if it means anything – cannot consist in what people like Metz and Moltmann think they have to understand by it: an apolitical Christianity. Belief has always been personal: you cannot believe for someone else or repent in his or her place. But that is not the same thing as making it a private matter, far less indicating that someone does not engage in politics. If people today claim that the church does not engage in politics, to its shame, in all probability they are claiming that it does not engage in politics as they understand it, namely left-wing politics.

So much for the misunderstanding that faith and politics have only been connected in our time. As we can see, there is a further misunderstanding behind this, that only left-wing politics is politics. So that we do not get led astray by the vagueness of the terms left and right a short digression would seem to me to be appropriate. It is quite possible that there was a time when left and right were meaningful descriptions of a political standpoint, but that time has now gone. The terminology is useful for propaganda and rousing emotions, for flag-waving and uniting one's own group (confirming its identity), but as soon as we try to fill it with content we get stuck. Is the left for democracy and against dictatorship? But there are also left-wing dictatorships. Are left-wing people less inclined to political violence than right-wing? That cannot be maintained either: there are also Red terror brigades. Censorship of the press is thought to be right-wing: bridling of the free expression of opinion. But more left-wing régimes have muzzled the press or even eliminated it than right-wing régimes. All that can be said, and it also applies to right-wing states, and if someone should say 'But that shows that a left-wing régime is not really left-wing', then right-wing governments may excuse themselves with precisely the same arguments. The instances can be repeated in connection with many other fundamentally political issues. Moreover, they show as clearly as one could desire that the terminology itself is being used as a weapon in the power struggle, in other words what matters is not what is said but what can be achieved by it in terms of gaining political power.

That is one of the reasons, the most obvious reason, why 'faith and politics' tends to be a murky question and, worse, falls victim in the political power struggle where talk has to be in terms of left and right. The second reason is already implied in the first: left and right no longer have any constitutive characteristics (except what people attribute to one another as a characteristic for reasons for propaganda) and can therefore stand for anything. The short summary that I have just given is irrefutable in that respect. The third reason follows on directly: by their use of propaganda 'left' and 'right' disguise the real controversies in politics. Mistakes must be talked down, changes blurred, since while the left can suffer a defeat it cannot be wrong and the same goes for the right.

The second misunderstanding, that only left-wing politics is politics, is also easily unmasked as being itself a political weapon. This is another reason, now from a practical political perspective, for maintaining that Christians need not be left-wing or socialist. 'Left-wing' and 'socialist' are too much *cartes blanches*, on which people can write what they like.

We have already come up against the other reasons why this need not be the case. The complete outlines of theology which have to demonstrate that left-wing politics follows from faith seem untenable. So the need to be left-wing or socialist does not follow from them.

That is not to say that it is impossible to be left-wing or socialist, in terms of the specific content of one's views. The only people to whom that would apply would be those who were afraid of political controversies. All that I am claiming is that theology must not be brought in to prove that the left and only the left fits the faith. Left-wing politics has no other criteria than right-wing or any other kind of politics for testing its credentials. What criteria are they?

The answer, as we again see, is at the same time the answer to the question why doing politics is a matter of faith for Christians.

The main aim towards which politics is struggling – packaged as a particular political ideal – is the well-being of the members of a society. At that point Christians concerned for change and conservative Christians are in agreement. Those concerned for change want to be conservative once their ideal has been realized to some degree and conservative Christians want change when the existing situation has departed too far from their ideal. That ideal is, if we describe it in as general terms as I did (the welfare of the members of a society), the same, apparently secular, political ideal for both.

Why it is a matter of faith for Christians to work for the realization of such a secular ideal and thus to engage in politics is already implied in this formulation. Christians do that with the same natural necessity (a necessity by-passing faith itself) as that with which they champion the neighbour at the level of personal relationship. Their faith means that they cannot require other than good for their neighbour (that which is good for him or her). They have not invented morality themselves: what is good is also known in other areas (there the doctrine of the two kingdoms is again an underlying factor). Morality formulates what has proved good for the other (maximal morality) or at least is not bad for him or her (minimal morality). Torture is never good for anyone, hence the rule that torture is always morally reprehensible: left-wing torture is as bad as right-wing torture. According to Jesus Christians do not abolish morality – Christians, too, hold one another and others to the rule not to torture – but then they go beyond the maximal morality: they do more than usual by discounting their own interest in some situations – an ingredient with which moral rules also reckon.

We have considered interpersonal action. But the furthering of the other's good calls not only for action on the level of interpersonal relationships; we also make use of the law, of the formation of political power and the regulation of social interests. If Christians are concerned for the welfare of others – and that is the case, as we saw – then they must also face questions like whether justice is being done to all citizens in a society, whether the social order which prevails there serves the welfare of people in such a way that one person does not get everything and the other nothing, and whether political power-relationships are regulated in such a way that at least some hold on power is given to all citizens and a great majority of them is not excluded, for whatever reason.

So we must see political and social commitment as a modern form of love of the neighbour. It does not make the classical form of this love, which appears everywhere in the Bible and the early Christian tradition – that from person to person, the only form that people knew – superfluous. The bowl of soup has to be brought, the chair for handicapped Mrs Smith has to be paid for and the work of the deacons has to be carried out – today more than ever. But we cannot love as we should today without politics and social commitment. This faith motivates Christians within the existing order to act according to the rule of love and therefore to further the welfare of others, but since we also have some – I deliberately say some – grip on the organization of this order and the political and social control of life in one way or another, together with others we too are morally responsible for this control. Thus Christians derive their engagement in politics from their faith, or more precisely, in the love of others their faith gives them the motive for political action. But that does not take us all the way. *What* must they do? Is faith also of help in establishing that? Or, to use the same words as in the second half of the basic question: have Christians any contribution to make to politics on the basis of their faith?

For more than one reason the answer to this question is not as simple as one might like. That is because political action is less simple than such a term suggests. Politics needs (*a*) principles; (*b*) an analysis of the situation in which these principles must be implemented; (*c*) an estimate of the consequences of decision A or step B; and (*d*) only if we have gone through all this are we in a position to give specific directives (as principles made operative in given situations) for political action. So what we are really asking is: Does faith give us any guidance – apart from the fact that it is a motive for political action – when we have to take these four steps that bring us to specific politics? I shall go through the whole series gradually and begin with political principles. Have we anything in faith which seeks political principles?

To answer this question I must first introduce a distinction into the term faith. This will make it clearer what we can and cannot do in politics. Faith is a term with many meanings, but two of them are important for us here: the faith that we believe and, distinct from that, the faith by which we believe. These are somewhat loose translations of the Latin terminology which is customary in theology, but the purpose of the distinction can easily be demonstrated. 'The faith by which we believe' is focussed on faith as an act or attitude of trust. Through faith Abraham went on a journey without knowing where he was going, and he is the model for it. To mention an even better known example, according to the apostle Paul we know that we are justified before God by faith and not by works of the law. Here faith amounts to entrusting oneself to what the message promises. Certain knowledge? Yes, certain knowledge. 'The faith that we believe' denotes the content of faith: what Christians believe. That God rescues the poor, has revealed himself in Jesus, is love and commands love – these are all expressions which, along with many others, make up the content of Christian faith, believed faith.

In the previous chapter I demonstrated in detail that the Bible and Christian tradition – taken together, the faith that is believed – contain more than 'the one Word of God, Jesus Christ'. God as creator comes into it just as much as does the salvation of creation and the knowledge of good and evil – the principles of humanity – as a fruit of cumulative human experience of the creation. Believed faith can therefore at the same time help Christians to formulate the basic principles for political action: raising up the poor from the mire, interceding for widows and orphans – i.e. the weak – feeding the hungry. Christians can get all this from their own tradition and generalize it into political principles. Of course we must be careful here. In the chapter about the social determination of Christian conceptions and concepts we could see how outdated social and political ideals creep in with these concepts and must therefore be purged if Christian conceptions and concepts are not to have an enslaving effect in the social and political sphere. We could not accept the discrimination against strangers which was customary in the ancient world (see e.g. Deut.15), much less the subordinate position of women which of course runs right through the Christian tradition (including the Bible) or withhold the law from slaves. So we cannot just act biblically, and fortunately do not do so. Moreover most people mean by 'biblical' not what is in the Bible but what they hold – with more or less justification – to be Christian.

Of course a further comment has to be made: the humanitarian principles from which we work in politics are not the property of the Christian tradition. As the wisdom of creation they stand in the Bible, but we also share them with others. They were there before the Bible was. Therefore strictly speaking it is unimportant whether they are taken from the Christian tradition or come from elsewhere, whether they have been formulated by Christians or non-Christians. You need not be a Christian to observe them. The critical question is sometimes whether we recognize (and can acknowledge) them as humanitarian principles. What conclusion must we draw? Politics always has to do with faith – in the sense of the faith that is believed – because and in so far as Christians see humanity as the criterion for political principles and the basic rules for humanity, although they can be got just as well outside Christianity from an integrating element of the Christian tradition of faith. Because these basic rules are at the same time shared by all – and are therefore universally human – it is possible to talk and work with others in connection with political principles. But that is a practical consequence which I shall leave aside here.

Now the contribution of believed faith, the Christian tradition, does not raise any problems as long as we keep political principles general: no exploitation of the poor and weak, no poverty, no violence or war; or in a more positive way: fair distribution of obligations and rewards, equal access to the law, power and the sources of prosperity and well-being, peace and sisterhood and so on. Such general principles or ends correspond closely to the universal human criteria for humanity. I have never met Christians who do not want a just society or a world where peace prevails.

But how are these conditions to be realized? The problems and controversies begin there.

So we need an analysis of the situation, since politics is always about realizing aims in a given situation. That involves in the first place knowing what is happening, knowledge of things. Why must something be done? Already at this point great problems arise: how much knowledge of things can we acquire? We are mostly dependent on the information of others and know *a priori* that this is not always unbiassed, and in many cases partisan knowledge is even used as a means of attaining power and influence. So what must we do with information? Anyone who is above unpartisan information is no longer welcome among supporters of a particular line precisely for that reason.

But that is only half the problem. Political analysis is also analysis of the conditions of power and this is again undertaken because it is necessary to see what measure will lead to what result. Is politics always concerned with results? We judge a political manoeuvre not by its good intentions but by its actual effect, since that is precisely why the manoeuvre is undertaken. If we allow good intentions to be a criterion, then any politics up to and including the politics of apartheid could be approved, since without doubt the South African government will vigorously produce evidence of its good intentions. But how do we know what effects a political action has? In a vacuum, that can be imagined: what you put in comes out again. But political situations are situations which are characterized by power relationships, and anyone who does not take that into account will be a catastrophe in politics: his or her ideals will be washed away or achieve the opposite of his or her (good) intentions. The analysis of power-relationships is therefore needed because we must estimate what effect a political decision or strategy has within a field of force that we ourselves have not made.

I shall use a specific topic to demonstrate the complication which arises if we want to move from general political principles – through analysis and estimates – to specific political directives for action: the struggle for peace. Today we are carrying on this struggle in a given situation which we have not created ourselves but which we must deal with, the situation in which nuclear weapons have created a balance of power between East and West, albeit a shaky balance. Moreover this balance has been achieved with the help of such devastating weapons that it is inconceivable that they would ever be used. What is the best service to peace in such a situation? Unilateral disarmament, removal of the balance of power? Or just continuing with threats? Is war likely to come from the positioning of cruise missiles (*Pravda*), will the positioning of them avoid war (Reagan) or does the positioning have no significance for either war or peace but only for the economy? I do not seek to settle the argument over cruise missiles with these simple questions but to show that in all these areas we are dealing with estimates, in other words raising questions which relate to the consequences of a particular measure, and not with political principles. Both the proponents and the opponents of cruise missiles want peace, but they have different views as to which measure will lead to the avoidance of a nuclear war and which will bring such a war closer. Estimates have a greater or lesser element of uncertainty. That can be reduced with the help of scientific investigation or forecasts on a scientific basis (war studies), but the margin of uncertainty remains in all political decisions which are taken within a field of force over which one has no control and where one is left to expectations and prognoses.

This brings me to an important question. If estimates are very difficult, cannot Christians do something with their faith in the second meaning of the word, faith as an act of trust? Again, I can best illustrate this question from the discussion of nuclear weapons. For an increasing number of Christians the struggle for peace has become a matter of faith in the sense that they will have nothing to do with assessments and estimates of consequences of a no-without-a-yes and want only to go by the compass of God's promise. That introduces risks, as they are well aware: one could see how unilateral disarmament could lead to the use of nuclear weapons. But they say that faith (as an act of trust) means that Christians may take deliberate risks which go beyond actual estimates. For believers it is in any case certain that such risks are not real risks since God will see that the trust of the believer is not put to shame. By accepting what others call risks, Christians can and must show the value of faith in politics.

The argument sounds compelling; it appeals to a basic element of faith: trust in God's power over all things. But it is untenable. Someone who has got into a minefield, has no map and therefore does not know which way to go, will certainly get blown up, faith and all, if he replaces calculation, estimation, exploration or whatever other means he still has at his disposal with believing trust in God's promises. That is like going up the fast lane of the motorway with your eyes closed. Such an undertaking not only punishes itself but is also untenable in the light of Christian faith. As an act of trust, believing can never be a substitute for questions about one's own responsibility, personal or collective, and this last also includes taking steps to protect oneself, calculating the possible consequences of measures, the risks that we run if we do something or do not do something and so on. No God or human being relieves us of this responsibility. That nuclear weapons must be banished from the world is a principle which we do not need Christian faith to agree with, although we can also teach it on the basis of Christian faith. But how this can and must happen without getting into a nuclear war – and nuclear weapons actually exist as a historical fact – is a matter of estimating risks. However, estimates can be disputed, mistakes can creep into them, the standpoint that one eventually takes is a product of rational considerations. Of course people may believe from this standpoint that something is in accordance with God's purposes, but that will not do away with mistakes in estimates, however tragic they may prove. In other words, what is being discussed is the estimate and not the faith that would leave something out and allow something else to be relevant. If Christians remember that in time, they can talk to one another in a more relativistic way about nuclear weapons than they have done so far.

Of course there is yet another reason why Christians must banish from their minds – I have good reasons for expressing myself so strongly – that the calculation of risks can be replaced in the political sphere by trust and faith. Political measures are collective measures: the effects relate to the whole and not just personally to believing Christians. If Christians want to run risks in their personal life through actions which only concern themselves, then we have to respect their views – at least if there are actions which affect only the agent himself or herself. Anyone who takes on suffering because of his or her faith – as trust – can become a sign for others. But in that case he or she does it voluntarily, as the one involved. To apply the pattern to the political level means to involve others unwillingly, perhaps against their will, in a decision of faith with far-reaching consequences. All the consequences of that are reason enough for

thinking again about whether one may make others share in the risk
which one's political standpoint involves. But if the consequences
are also consequences of a decision of faith, the resultant risk is not
something that one can impose on non-believers. That comes near
to compulsion, and worse: it presents Christianity as a political force
which can be used for domination where it has the power. That is
at least anti-propaganda for believers since they cannot accept any
compulsion, certainly not the compulsion of the formation of
political power.

I shall sum up this chapter in the form of a conclusion with a
number of notes. Because politics involves not only having ideals
but also being able to implement those ideals; because estimating
political results is even more difficult and ambiguous than exercising
power, the connection between politics and faith is also not as simple
as, or at any rate is less simple than, is often supposed. I am not
talking about the ideals and the basic political principles. They
present no problems; they lend themselves readily towards showing
the flag. But things become more difficult as we progress. Faith may
be the motive for political action, may provide basic principles, but
everything is less clear when it comes to concrete directives. Practice
also indicates that Christians continue to hold different political
standpoints in almost all important political matters. Although they
have their faith in the background, the directives are clearly open
to discussion.

How does it come about that we do not find it so easy to elevate
political standpoints into standpoints of faith and at the same time
will not or cannot let go of the fact that politics is to do with faith?

I shall give a number of reasons to explain this situation and at
the same time show that it is unavoidable and that it thus disturbs
Christian politics.

1. We have already come across a first reason: politics is indeed
concerned with ideals, principles and aims which have to be realized,
but what matters in politics is the result: a politician or a party which
has many ideals, even Christian ideals, in its programme of action
but realizes none of them is pushed aside. We have formed parties
and elected politicians to get things done, in other words for results,
and their competence is demonstrated by the results they get.

However, it is far from certain what measure will have what
result. The other factors which determine the outcome are many,

unforeseeable and often incalculable. The situation must be assessed and a directive given on the basis of the assessment, but there can be differences of opinion over both the situation and the directive, though everyone is agreed about the aim to be achieved: no poverty for the lowest paid, peace in the world and so on. That gives every political measure, every directive, every subsidiary aim the character of what I have called an estimate. Christians, as I have shown, cannot avoid the problem of uncertainty that is involved with estimates by a leap of faith and that means that Christians, too, cannot be as certain as they would like to be about the directives and subsidiary aims they have derived from faith.

2. In the second place politics is practised in a world of violence and the struggle for power. Therefore a definition of politics which says nothing about the power struggle does not say much. Politics exists precisely because power is needed to realize ideals. However, that means that engaging in politics irrevocably and inextricably leads to a struggle for power and in a power struggle the directives that had been set up are not always followed. Might must be answered with might, violence in most cases with counter-violence. In that case I am envisaging the worst, but even if politics is done in a more moderate way the world depends on political choices and compromises. There is no politics without dirty hands. That too is part of politics and just as we cannot do without politics, so we cannot do without compromises. That is a hard truth which we see confirmed every day in practice. It would not need to be if our world were an ideal one, but it is not. In an ideal world the wolf would not eat the lamb but in our world that happens, and we have to find a way to stop it happening: by making the wolf a lamb (impossible), making the lamb a wolf (also impossible), protecting the lamb (that is better) or restraining the wolf (also possible). To make a mistake in the measure means that the lamb immediately gets eaten up.

We do not live in an ideal world, and there is no point in constructing an ideal world and making directives with its help. Wolves eat up lambs – that is a truth of experience. To construct an ideal world in which things which should not happen may not happen gives no support for action in a world in which things happen other than those which ought to happen, but we all know that. Moreover ethics is not a matter of formulating ideals but of making as good a decision as possible in the existing world with its existing alternatives.

That is the service which ethics can also show to politics in formulating aims (basic principles), sub-aims and modes of action and
criticizing them: not providing ideal worlds and ideal forms of
society.

There is nothing typically Christian in this last. Apart from the
unavoidable fact that any ideal is taken out of thin air – who knows
what is ideal? – we can establish that Christians in particular should
be suspicious about ideal societies precisely because of their faith.
Not only because paper is patient or paper worlds have no inherent
power to change but above all because ideal worlds with ideal people
and ideal norms imply a fundamental mistake about real people and
the real world and therefore also a fundamental mistake in the
strategy for changing evil. The last mistake is the one with the most
consequences: anyone who underestimates the wolf makes lambs
wolf-fodder. But that is enough on that point. There are no ideal
politics in a world which is not ideal, nor any ideal politics, not even
ideal politics by or through faith.

3. What I have just said has already moved us on to the aspect of
faith which most hampers action (political action): people are not
ideal people (not even Christians who act in faith). They come into
conflict and do so above all when the struggle for power, prestige
and interest is sparked off.

That is a form of sober realism which Christian faith introduces
into politics with its view of humanity. The Christian view of man is
not optimistic, so Christians must not have any illusions about
themselves, about others, or about the world of social and political
struggle. What can be achieved can be formulated better in negative
than in positive terms: if we see a chance to achieve less injustice,
less racial hatred, less hunger, less political terror, in a word less
shedding of tears than before, we may talk of success.

The ambiguity of political action is our ambiguity as people. That
is another reason why as soon as we talk about specific politics it is
less easy to associate politics with faith than we would like. Perhaps
our ancestors with their doctrine of two kingdoms were not so stupid
and its deepest roots lie here. They may well have seen how
vulnerable political action is, how much happens there which does
not pass muster and which nevertheless must happen and then wisely
resolved not to compromise the God of the gospel of Christ with it
and at the same time not withdraw the whole field from faith. That

became, was, and is the doctrine of two kingdoms: a summary of the irrevocable ambiguity of Christian existence.

A last question: can Christian faith still be critical and radical? That does not seem to me to have been in any way questioned by the interpretation that I have given of it. But to be safe, I shall add a number of comments.

1. Emotions about poverty, natural disaster, political violence, oppression or whatever else may befall us are familiar to everyone. Christian faith sharpens one's eye – if it is good – for suffering and injustice and in this sense arouses the emotions. But these are as it were experiences of contrast. They are conditions for criticism but do not coincide with it. For criticism, criteria of a social and political kind are needed. Experiences of contrast can only become serious criticism when they become social and political criteria, but not all experiences of contrast can be that,

2. Radical criticism from faith is indeed possible – though the necessary criteria are mostly lacking – but it continues to have an inner contradiction because it always rebounds on the one who criticizes. For the means for changing society the critic is directed back to what he criticizes. So he perpetuates society while he changes it. Radical criticism is therefore either pseudo-holy or it is less radical than it seems.

3. A person is critical because he wants to protect something that must not be lost. Otherwise criticism would be senseless. Criticism is thus concerned with preservation and as such is never annihilating criticism, unless someone does not know what he or she wants to preserve. But Christian faith is well aware of that: the existing world as God's creation. Therefore the priority is given to what is above what is not. To be Christian is to be more than critical.

4. Criticism takes its criteria from the existing world; they are not eschatological criteria. We can of course elevate our this-worldly criteria to being an eschatological force, but if we do that we are still the same people and can only talk about the eschaton in terms of the present: the trappings of the Last Awakening come to us through the present day. We do not know what we shall be.

5. The first-fruits of God's coming kingdom in the present are the forgiveness of sins and life through the Spirit of God. We can speak of first-fruits in an unusual sense or first-fruits in conditions of our old world where tears are wiped away. But everything has its price.

Wiping away tears brings new tears, which we cannot discount or make good in this world unless new tears flow, and so on.

6. Criticism which is made by Christian faith – as an act of trust and as believed faith – is characterized by the fact that it can accept the disappointments of history because it knows that the history of the world is not the judgment of the world.

Bibliography

W.Benjamin, *Zur Kritik der Gewalt und andere Aufsätze*, Frankfurt 1971

C.Bussmann, *Befreiung durch Jesus? Die Christologie der latein-amerikanischen Befreiungstheologie*, Munich 1980

J.de Graaf, 'Doel, middel en bedoeling en hun ethische relatie', *Nieuw theologisch Tijdschrift* 31, 1977, 46-56

J.Heckel, *Im Irrgarten der Zwei-Reich-Lehre*, Munich 1957

M.Hengel, 'Das Ende aller Politik. Die Bergpredigt in der aktuellen Diskussion (I)', *Evangelische Kommentare* 12, 1981, 686-90

M.Hengel, 'Die Stadt auf dem Berge. Die Bergpredigt in der aktuellen Diskussion (II)', *Evangelische Kommentare* 1, 1982, 19-22

L.Kolakowski, *Main Currents of Marxism. I, The Founders; III, The Breakdown*, Oxford University Press 1981

H.M.Kuitert, 'De rol van de bijbel in de protestantische theologische etiek', *Gereformeerd theologisch Tijdschrift* 81, 1981, 65-82

H.M.Kuitert, 'Kan politiek Messiaans zijn?', *Gereformeerde Week-blad* 38, 1982, 12, 19, 26 March and 2, 9 April

E.Leroy Long, *A Survey of Recent Christian Ethics*, Oxford University Press, New York 1982

I.Lipschits, *Links en rechts in de politiek*, Meppel 1969

J.Miguez Bonino, *Toward a Christian Political Ethics*. Fortress Press, Philadelphia and SCM Press 1983

A.W.Musschenga, *Noodzakelijkheid en mogelijkheid van moraal*, Amsterdam and Assen 1981

R.Niebuhr, *Moral Man and Immoral Society*, Scribner, New York 1932 and SCM Press 1963

J.Outka and J.P.Reader (eds.), *Religion and Morality*, New York 1973

W.Schmithals, 'Jesus und die Weltlichkeit des Reiches Gottes', *Evangelische Kommentare* I, 1968, 313-20

H.Scholl, *Reformation und Politik. Politische Ethik bei Luther, Calvin und den Frühhugenotten*, Stuttgart and Berlin 1976

W.Teichert, *Mussen Christen Sozialisten sein?*, Hamburg 1976

Mady Thung et al., *Naar de toekomst leven*, Baarn 1977

R.Veldhuis, *Realism versus Utopianism?*, Assen 1975

C.Walther, *Theologie und Gesellschaft*, Zurich and Stuttgart 1967

T.Witvliet, *The Way of the Black Messiah*, SCM Press 1986

V What the Church Says

15. The politicizing of the church

This new chapter is about adaptation. It presupposes the previous analyses and arguments and will tie the loose ends together into a pattern that can help us to distinguish between what we mean and what we do not mean.

To begin with a direct question: do we mean to politicize the church or have we allowed ourselves to be lulled to sleep too easily by people for whom politics is everything to such a degree that they even want to blow up the church in so far as it cannot brought under the yoke of politics? By politicizing the church I do not mean the church being involved in politics. That is too general and unqualified a description which runs parallel to the general descriptions of politics that we met in Part I. Politics is more than having a deep concern for society. If that is the whole story, then we must immediately apply the term politics to church, faith and theology. But such inappropriate definitions get us nowhere. Politics has to do with ideals, as we have seen, and with the struggle for power to realize these ideals. Without the latter element we have not got to politics. With the help of this I shall now define what politicizing the church means in this chapter: politicizing means what we understand by it when we say that a UNICEF conference or a conference of Women in the World has been politicized, namely that it has become involved in the power struggle for realizing political ideals, voluntarily or involuntarily. This last point is not relevant to the definition of politicizing: one thus becomes or is a political subject which takes part in strategies aimed at getting or keeping power.

It is also necessary for us not to be mistaken about the word church. By it I mean the church as an organized form of Christian faith, i.e. the church as an institution, and not believers, Christians or church people. What is the difference? The church as an institution is the community of believers as they explain themselves in faith, as people of God, new creation, including its official organization (synods, priests, bureaux, councils and so on) by which it presents a different aspect to a society from other organizations. It is taken to include all members: when the synod speaks (or in the Roman Catholic church, the Pope), the church speaks. I need not say more at this point: I am simply concerned with the practical difference between church people, church members and believers on the one hand and the church on the other. If this chapter is concerned about the politicizing of the church, I do not mean the individual members or believers who take part in politics – as far as I am concerned they cannot do enough in that direction – but the church as an institution which has become involved in the political power struggle.

The first question is whether that is the case. Is the church entangled in the power struggle? To answer this question we must turn to what people call 'what the church says', not just speaking, or preaching the gospel, but making statements about political and social questions. As an example I shall take the statements that the various churches in the Netherlands have made about the possession and use of nuclear weapons to and with the authorities – through the synods of the Reformed churches – in order to prevent the positioning of cruise missiles. There have also been other statements about tricky matters in the social sphere. Thus the Netherlands Council of Churches has recently tackled the government over its policy in connection with giving up social minima and replacing them with a better policy. Let me give a couple of examples. They can be supplemented by many others, both from the Netherlands and elsewhere, for example Germany. I mention that country deliberately because especially in West Germany and in the Netherlands the effect was the same: a colossal polarization developed within the churches between supporters and opponents of the statements. They were almost writing on the wall. Even the supporters of the statements of the church – which is how from now on I shall abbreviate political statements of the church – have to say that. It is inconceivable that such fierce polarization, which was so painful as far as the public side of the church was concerned – should have had no deeper background than that of an ordinary dispute. Why are political statements in the churches so divisive? I shall give a number of reasons for this, which eventually justify the conclusion that the church has indeed been drawn into the political struggle.

The first point is that political statements are on questions which

relate to society. Usually such questions are solved by the formation
of political power groups in parliament. This formation of power
groups is done by means of political parties which have come into
being for precisely this aim: there is an ideal, there are aims, and in
order to have these realized a political party is set up with a political
programme which tries to get as many people as possible to join it.
That is how political power develops in a democratic society like
our own. I stress that here for two reasons: party politics is not a
vice, no matter how much scandal may surround party politics.
Anyone who wants to kill off parliamentary democracy need only
turn his back on party politics. Secondly (and this is my concern),
only if we see that social questions in a parliamentary democracy
are solved by the establishment of party political power, do we see
the implication of statements by the church. In a society like ours,
a church which expresses itself through official statements about
controversial political and social questions automatically falls into
one political category or another. There is no escaping this unless
the statements are put in the most general way possible and are
therefore as vague as possible. But those who are keen that the
church should make statements – often the church leaders themselves – are against precisely that. What is left is that by speaking
out, the churches can only approve or reject, and in so doing make
their entry into the political arena. Whether they belong there or
not is, of course, another question which I shall discuss later. For
the moment I need go no further than that we find here a first
explanation of the extremely fierce and disruptive polarization: by
making statements the church enters the sphere of politics and
politics enters the church.

But there is more to it than that. The church approves certain
political standpoints, but is it really the church that is speaking?
Which church? We do not know *the* church; all we know is churches
(in the plural) each of which proclaims that it is the church, since
otherwise it could not be the church making a statement. But of
course they are only part of the church and, moreover, a part of the
church in part of the world, for example the Netherlands. That
relativizes considerably what the church says. However, that is still
not the whole story, for how can the church really speak if a
particular church community is speaking? Perhaps the Roman
Catholic church may have psychological questions to solve here, but

it has none relating to canon law. Anyone who is or becomes a Roman Catholic accepts the leadership of the church by one head, the Pope, supported by the bishops. That is the way Roman Catholic canon law has it. For most of the Reformation churches things are different. From the beginning they also have had control of canon law, which is regulated by the authorities in church councils and synods. Through elections the church council is the local church and through indirect elections delegates are elected to the synods of the church, provincially or nationally. But can that still be maintained today? Law – including church law – represents nothing (and cannot go on being practised) if it has no *Sitz im Leben* for the implementation of the law. That has long since been the case in the churches, for many reasons but in any case also because of the shift in our sense of law. We feel that a government which is not democratically elected and which as a result does not arrive at decisions or make statements in a democratic way is not a government. If the resolutions and statements further concern politics, this seems to be further evasion since we instituted democracy in the first place for making political statements and passing resolutions.

I am not arguing that the churches should be given a kind of democratic structure nor do I believe that truth or falsehood should be established through democratic decisions. The one thing I want to say is that when the church government speaks – and it is in fact the voice of the church – no church member can have the feeling of being represented by this leadership, and at the same time the leadership says things that many church members can interpret only as approval of a party and group of which they themselves would never approve. That can only result in an extremely unsatisfactory sense of law, particularly among those people who are at odds with it (and that means – if such talk goes on – are directly opposed to it). I have been talking about the churches (and thus really church communities). Whereas synods and church councils can still in some sense appeal to church law for their statements, the World Council of Churches and the Netherlands Council of Churches lacks any appearance of legitimation. That is extremely painful, since the World Council of Churches is concerned with world politics and the Netherlands Council of Churches with politics in our own country: they hold discussions about political matters with the authorities, send delegations and so on. The point is not that these Councils do not have political freedom to do this. Who would want to prevent them from talking about politics or discussing politics with the authorities? Certainly not the authorities. Whether they attach any importance to these statements is another matter. That the authorities themselves must know.

Nor is the point that the expressions or delegations are nonsensical or quite perverse. Of course they could be, but that is not the presupposition from which I start. What I am concerned with is that they are in the name of the churches and that there is no legal basis for this from the perspective of church law. That should stick in the churches' throat. If it is to have any meaning, 'The church says' can only mean all the church, but that is not the case. The voice is that of a church community and within that church community of a small group of leading figures. That is the actual situation. When we read in the paper that 'the churches' are speaking out for a particular measure or that an organization or a government has turned the spotlight on 'the churches' then we need not be afraid. This relates to a small tip of – shall we say – knowledgeable people, but they are not 'the churches'. If we couple this result with the previous analysis, it appears that in 'what the church says' a group of church leaders approves one or more party-political standpoints which are presented by our parliamentary democracy. Thus the church is not really entering the political arena but is slipped in by the church leaders through the political statements that they make. If we want to think of the church or church community in terms of the people, the basic community, the ordinary people and not the élite, then what is said is often against their views.

Does this politicize the church in the sense of involving it in the political power struggle? I think that the earlier analyses confirm this position with all the clarity that could be desired. The polarization which I indicated at the beginning of this section is a consequence of this. From a political perspective the making of statements by the church means that the authority of the church is bestowed on party-political standpoints, often the standpoints of the small group of leaders who make declarations and send delegations. Here synods and councils make the churches a factor in the power struggle, a pressure group, the subject – and indeed the object and often the plaything – of those concerned for political power. From the perspective of power politics, politicians are always glad to have the churches on their side, although the church may be of no further interest to them otherwise. The politicians must not be criticized for this: without power they cannot realize any of their aims. But the churches must be wiser and not want this deliberately. What the church says is not a political question but a problem for the church and we must put this question to the churches by asking whether they really want to enter into the heritage of politics and thus politicize the church. I see this tendency as the fruit of a perhaps unconscious enterprise of the politicizing of life, to which the churches also bow the knee. Is everything politics? Then so are the churches.

In theological terms Karl Barth's doctrine of the church gives us an opening here. What makes the church the church is hearing the Word of God in the person of Jesus Christ. The church does not know more and does not need to know more, since the Word of God says everything that the church needs to live. Here, as we have seen, Barth goes against the classical conception that God makes known his will, and especially his will for social life, through creation and nature. However, according to Barth, no knowledge of God may be got from there. For this knowledge we cannot go anywhere other than to the one Word, Jesus Christ.

Barth himself drew the far-reaching consequences of this doctrine (the one Word of God). Is that one Word preached and believed by the church? In that case we too must be in the church to know God's will, not only for the mutual dealings of Christians within the church, but also for the social and political order.

It was this view of the church which became very popular from the 1950s on, especially among the theologians of the Western world, though not with any reference to Barth. The preference for this view is understandable: it settles the question of knowledge without dualism: above all we must be in Jesus Christ and thus in the church which knows of God's revelation in Jesus. In Barth, of the two kingdoms only the church is left; in fact for him everything not only revolves around the church, but the church is the only sphere; moreover it may be that sphere because it begins with itself, it is the real world. Culture and work are *parergon* (*par-* by and *ergon* = work); the church and covenant are *ergon*, as we can read in his *Church Dogmatics*.

This view of the church elevates the church's understanding of itself to an enormous degree: with the proclamation of Jesus Christ as its real and only task it has the Word of redemption in its midst. If it has no idea how social and political problems, for example the problems of armament and disarmament, are to be solved, who does have? I am not claiming – very far from it – that by this doctrine Barth lent support to the politicizing of the church: that is why I said that his teaching provided an opening for it. What I am arguing is that this teaching was used for that: the church knows it, the church may say it in all freedom, without paying any attention to the world, for the church does not begin where the world begins, but begins with itself. Politicizing (in the definition which I gave) is the ruin of the Christian church. I shall sum up why in a number of points.

1. Politicizing brings the church into contradiction with its interpretation of itself. That can be illustrated from the current concept of power. Why must the church speak on social and political questions? Because there is a social presupposition to the statements that it makes: it is a significant factor, an ideological apparatus (to use the terms of Althusser), and such a factor – as Marxists too have discovered – represents power. The church which makes statements (viz. the church leaders) is also aware of that, otherwise it would not speak. We have seen that about the church from the outside.

What is the justification for such statements from within the church? Again, power, but now power in the spiritual sense. According to the church's interpretation of itself the power which it has is the power in which it believes, the power of the Holy Spirit which authorizes it to speak. So there are two kinds of power, power in the sociological sense (control of the means of controlling others) and power in the spiritual sense (the light and power of the Spirit of God), secular and spiritual power. As we know today, both kinds of power are misused in what the church says: the worldly power of the church is used with an appeal to its spiritual power (the illumination of the Spirit) in order to help political and social standpoints to worldly power. Here, however, the Christian church is forced to be untrue to itself. As a church it knows no other power than faith and it can fight only with the sword of the Spirit. If it brings its spiritual power into worldly power-play, then it irrevocably becomes a political subject, as we have seen, a party in politics, or a political party – and then it is no longer the church. In that case must no political battles be fought for the realization of social and political ends? Of course they must, but they must be carried on by Christians, church people, and not by the church. Let me recall the distinction which I made in this connection at the begining of this chapter. The doctrine of the two kingdoms was not a pointless invention. Christians are not just members of the church but also partners in the secular kingdom, the kingdom of the creation approved by God. So they are also involved – in the name of God, as they must be – in the power struggle in the political arena by means of the institutions that exist there. But the church cannot be involved there without being unfaithful to that which makes it the church, life from the Spirit which makes it a new creation.

2. Politicization saddles the church with a role for which it is not equipped. As church, the church must not only not want to be a political subject, it *cannot* be; it lacks the skill and the instruments for acquiring this knowledge. Moreover in reality it can fulfil this role much less well than church leaders think. Certainly nuclear weapons must be got rid of, but church leaders do not know any better than politicians what political steps are useful for achieving that. What the church thinks it has to say about politics and social solutions is therefore either so general that it does not amount to anything or is something that has already been said elsewhere. As we have seen, it takes its options from political parties and trends which are in fact equipped for political business and does not begin with itself – as if there were no world. It cannot do otherwise; that is where it comes from.

Then can the church not speak prophetically? After all, the prophets of the Old Testament were authorized to speak to the authorities of those days in the name of God and to give political instructions. That is true; the Old Testament prophets were involved in politics, indeed in a very specific way, and they were so in the name of the One who sent them. Synods and preachers in the Netherlands could be similarly involved, since church and state coincide there, but they are not, nor should they be. In political terms the Israel of the Old Testament was a theocracy: the people and the people of God coincided. We do not live in a theocracy: that is the difference. Therefore in our society churches and church leaders cannot give prophetic instructions about politics. If 'prophetic' means in the name of the One who sends them, that is not only dangerous (who controls it?) but also very suspect: in this way the church protects its statements from criticism and thus makes itself right *a priori*. So it forfeits its place as a serious discussion partner. If it does not set prophetic speaking over against insight and counsel but makes use of them too, then would it not be quite possible to get along only with insight and counsel? So it is hard to see why the term prophetic should still be used. Suppose we take the view that no cruise missiles should be positioned in the Netherlands. Is that a prophetic statement? Many atheists and indeed completely atheistic organizations have arrived at the same conclusion and say the same thing. So do we need a Christian church to make prophetic statements? If that is the case, the word changes its meaning and simply indicates that we find a statement good or agree with it, and there must then be reasons why one clearly need not be a Christian to be able to see that. That makes it quite clear that political attitudes do not follow directly from prophetic light or insight: political insight comes first; it was there already and was later given prophetic clothing.

The same goes for political reading of the Bible. Doubtless that can make a contribution, in making us read the Bible very differently from the way in which we are accustomed, but it does not make us that much wiser. The political ideas are already there, and the eyes with which we read are already directed by them. Then we go on to read the Bible. The Bible does not bring us to political positions and options; the Bible confirms them and we find them in the Bible or read them into it and so on. Exegesis becomes illustration.

Moreover what really happens in political statements and reading the Bible is rather different: the church duplicates in religious terms what has already been discovered or stated with the help of some political statements. Why? Who or what is helped or advanced by this duplication? Political trends, authorities or would-be authorities? Or is it the church – the churches – itself that is returning to the theocratic ideal that God communicates his will for political and social life to the world through its ministers? Anyone involved in the power struggle needs power. That also applies to the church. But it is bad for the churches. There is already far too much compulsion and ambition to dominate in the churches. Must the political power struggle be there too? A church which is concerned for power is the revenge of the doctrine of the one Word of God.

3. The politicizing of the church brings politics in political style

into the church. The church is politicized in a bad sense: it changes its own rules of conduct for those with which people deal with one another in the political sphere. That means internal chaos. Let me explain what I mean with a few examples. Politics is a power struggle, of course on behalf of a good aim – we may assume – but it is nevertheless a power struggle. Now we can read that Machiavelli brought his own rules to the power struggle and that these rules – as Machiavelli in fairness related them – are irreconcilable with the Christian love of neighbour and love of the truth. In politics you cannot love the least significant, cannot let the other go first, cannot forgive and begin again (unless that gives you power), cannot think the other more excellent than yourself (at least, you can never say that), for those who do that sort of thing give away power which they never get back. In politics you must show how good you are, walk at the front of demonstrations, love meetings, see yourself (and praise yourself) as being far better than others. In politics you give your opponent a push if he almost falls rather than helping him; you do not let anything go his way, you seize what you can in order to put the other party in a bad light. And so far I have not got to Machiavelli's other prophecy: a prince who speaks the truth will not last long. Politics means struggle, self-glorification and intolerance with the aim of acquiring or keeping power. All that comes within the church if we politicize it (make it share in the political power struggle), so we have nothing to expect but hate, jealousy, envy, lovelessness and self-glorification! We can see it taking place before our eyes in the phenomenon of polarization: the floor is swept of political opponents. The attitude of 'holier than thou' has to be brought into the church; the one who does not share my political preference becomes like a tax collector and publican and one does not speak to him. And Christianity falls apart into two halves, good and bad, the servants of others and the servants of their own interests – the opposite side are always the latter. Things are as they were in the time of the conventicles, except that these have now become political conventicles, the church is the mass which must be written off, and the small group has life and truth in itself. So ultimately the sombre definition proposed by Carl Schmitt will become truth in the church: politics is disputing with your enemies since only in and through politics do you come to know who your enemies are.

Here too I stress that we need not play off political activity against the church. There must be politics, but we must not have too many illusions about the way in which they are carried on. And above all, this way of doing politics must not find its way into the church, if all relationships are not to enter the lovelessness of politics. Politics politicizes the church and makes it a ruin.

4. Moreover politicizing turns politics into the church. The more the churches take part in the formation of specific political resolutions, the less significant existing political institutions become, from political parties up to the government.

That follows from the theology of the one Word of God: if the church begins with itself and is really the world, then politics can also regularly be practised from the church, by-passing all the regulations that we have so far built up to control the political power struggle. To put it more strongly, to interfere in these regulations brings the church under the suspicion of setting up another Lord, and conversely, confessing the one Lord implies that there need no longer be any respect for authority or state. The latter are rather to be criticized and disputed and not to be used as a means of making society more just. Moreover a number of Christians find it quite natural to make a direct connection between the Word that looks for faith and political action, in other words, without more ado to practise politics directly from the church. In this way of thinking the church has become completely a substitute for existing institutions. Therefore what in classical theology is called church and state or church and authority now becomes church and politics. The intermediary institutions which stood between faith and politics fall out.

I see that as a development which can have fatal consequences for the practice of politics. We evacuate politics of significance if we do politics through church channels, and in this way contribute rather to the decline of what we wanted to preserve, parliamentary democracy. Christians can contribute to the decline if they politicize the church and make it do what is the work and the responsibility of political organs. The shrivelling up of political institutions which is the consequence of that is one thing. What we get in its place, however, is not real politics. It is something else. Church assemblies can give advice and express whatever views they like, but they have no political responsibility for them. Political parties come to grief, politicians are deposed; that is the way in which wrong politics is punished. There is no way of punishing wrong political advice and statements by the churches. No one is responsible, no one can be deposed; everything is – in political terms – free. That is the frustration of politics.

What does this chapter add up to? Not to the view that Christians must not be involved in politics. In the previous Parts, but also again in this chapter, I have shown that as Christians they have to be. They must not be afraid of the power struggle, something which some will find more and others less difficult, where it is a matter of achieving justice, preserving the environment, banishing discrimination and so on. But the church *qua church* will lose itself if it takes part in this struggle. Does the Christian church *qua church* then do nothing when it comes to politics? That would be the wrong conclusion to draw. In an emergency – that is the first indication – it must try. By emergency I mean a situation in which the gaining of power through political parties is forbidden or political parties do not exist. South Africa is a good example: who is to give a voice and support to the oppressed blacks and coloureds if they themselves may not gain power through party and parliament? Many examples could be given. In such situations the churches may and indeed must try to give a voice to those who have none. But what if the situation is not an emergency? Then the main standpoint of this chapter is that politics must be done through politics and not through church channels. Each must have its own place. The church is the church and must not want to become involved with the authorities or take part in the power struggle between political parties, any more than the authorities or the political parties can ever or must ever take the place of the church.

A second comment: politics must not be done within the church in a political way, but to be involved in them in the style of the church is not only permissible but has also been enjoined and practised as long as the Christian church has existed. Humanitarian principles form an essential element of its preaching and instruction. Oppression, exploitation, discrimination may not happen anywhere, and may not even be practised by the God of the Christian church. Granted, that comes close to a generalization. Except in exceptional situations, the churches can do no more than that. The criterion for oppression, when is it to be applied, how you deal with oppressors – all that calls for consideration in which Christians must put their best foot forward, but churches are not equipped for answering that sort of question.

In times of great political controversies – and this is my third comment – the church can let politics into the church in yet another way, namely by providing for Christians who are political opponents the platform they need on which they can talk clearly to each other about their different views without feeling the hot breath of prestige, the power struggle and political success on their necks. Had the Christian church done that in South Africa, things would never have got into the state they are in now. I have written elsewhere about these matters at length, so I will not go into them further here.

Is the church still credible if it does not engage in politics in a world in which politics is service? The question is worth considering. Many political statements and actions by churches are produced for the motive of being (and remaining) credible. A church which does not want to burn its fingers over matters of earthly salvation (well-being) cannot be a church which instils respect for its message of eternal salvation.

This last point is certainly true. Being ready to burn one's figures (and not to think that you are doing so) is also a useful criterion for what I have called emergency situations. But here we must not lose sight of several things. Credibility is the problem of the messenger and not of the message: a messenger cannot change his or her message to become credible. The messenger must change himself or herself, since that is where the shoe pinches. Moreover a Christian church must without any apology move towards having a real interest in the social and political future of people in the midst of whom it functions as a church, if it has not been interested in that direction so far. But apart from the emergency situations which I have just mentioned, need it do that by means of political statements and positions? The Christian church has more arrows to its bow. It has its own diaconal care which is irreplaceable, and is all the more so the more it can help people outside the political struggle. It has its preaching of God's commands and promises. It also has its intercessions. All that cannot be got anywhere else, but only in the church, and only in the church do people know – or should people know – what that is worth. Living people share the life of their world and they can make that contribution to it. That means arousing emotions: perplexity, anger, bewilderment, disappointment, sorrow. And arousing political and social emotions. Christians living in two kingdoms bring these emotions into the church and there they are given a special place. In its prayers the Christian world opens up the world to God. It does not ask him for any solutions, but it commends itself and the world to him. That is how politics is done in the church's way in the church.

16. The socializing of faith

It is not that the church must be involved in politics: it would ruin itself if it were. However, church members must be. That was the drift of the last chapter. In this chapter and the next the perspective shifts: church members must be involved in politics, actually on the basis of their faith, but if they think that politics is everything, they will ruin faith itself.

Is there any reason for assuming that Christians think that? There is indeed, as we shall see in a moment. Just as one particular theology – I am still using the term in the sense of an outline proclamation – offers an opening for the politicizing of the church, so too there is a theology which gives the impression (to put it gently) that faith ends up in politics. I shall use a different term for that and speak of the socializing of faith. But before I go on to an explanation of what I mean by that, first of all I must describe the theology which is at the root of it.

In the theology of Karl Barth the church which makes political statements has found a theology to legitimate its words and actions: the doctrine of the one Word of God, spoken in Jesus Christ. There are not two Words: everything is said in Jesus. We do not need other authorities (nature and creation) even for directives, for example those for social and political action; according to Barth, we would not find them there: the one Word is enough. That Word must be preached and believed in the church: in that case we must go to the church for political advice.

Moltmann and, in his footsteps, a number of European and Latin-American theologies of liberation build on the foundation of this theology. But at the same time it undergoes an important change. The one Word, Jesus Christ, continues to be the starting point. But it is now no longer seen as the Word which has taken place but as the Word which will take place one day. Karl Barth had a fine sense of the theological earthquake which was happening before his eyes at the end of his life. 'I don't understand you,' he wrote in a letter to Gollwitzer, for years his pupil and comrade who was slowly moving over to political theology, 'I don't understand you: do you really want to move from "it has happened" to "it has still to happen"?' I am not quoting him literally, but this is the gist of what he means. In fact Barth hits the nail on the head: that was the intention. The message (the outline proclamation) of the one Word Jesus Christ is not that God has established himself once for all with his salvation in our world but that he will establish himself in it soon, in the future. Anyone who says Jesus says another world, and given that there is only one Word of God, as believers we need not say anything but Jesus, who brings that other world. Faith becomes expectation of the future.

In the previous Parts we were able to go into theological construction at length. I shall not repeat what I said there, but simply refer to the points that we need here. For example, expectation of the future is in itself nothing new: this has always been a fixed element of the Christian outline proclamation. The Book of Revelation ends with the vision of a new heaven and a new earth, with the annihilation of the devil and death and the wiping away of all tears. But that was not the only thing that the Christian outline proclamation had to say: it also spoke of creation, of God's guidance in our life, of forgiveness and the indwelling of the Spirit – to mention just a few key themes which everyone will know. The new factor is that the message of salvation, the one Word of Jesus Christ, is limited to the Word of the future and that faith is therefore limited to faith in the future.

Now there are great difficulties in this concentration of Christian faith on future belief, as we have already seen. All political theologies wrestle with them.

To proclaim the coming kingdom is not just to proclaim the future, or even future salvation, but to the degree that this future is different from our world, it is primarily and above all else critical; the more it puts the accent on 'the other', the more radical the criticism is. Revelation from God is almost the same thing as criticism from God. In itself that is again nothing new. Anyone who looks at the classical outline proclamation will soon discover that radical criticism from God appears there, too. This already begins with the apostle Paul, when we hear him say that no man is justified before God.

But in that case – and here is the difference – we have criticism from God of man as a sinner. The radical criticism of political theology is political criticism. The other world of God – the kingdom – has political features and is also developed in terms of recognizable political reality. This world is radically different because injustice, compulsion, violence and exploitation have given place to freedom, collaboration and the sisterhood of all people. Is this a Christian utopia? We might well call it that. But as happens with all utopias, how far away from us is it? Can we reach it, or must we keep to the literal meaning of the word, nowhere?

There are in principle three ways open here to the Christian proclamation of salvation, along with all the intermediate ways that people might want to add. We have already come across two of them; the third is new. One can make the proclamation of the coming kingdom of God begin and end with radical total criticism of this world. It cannot go further in the light of the gospel. That is possibility number one. It is not satisfactory; that is almost obvious. It makes no sense then for deciphering our world: that does not become the kingdom of God. However, what must we do? If it can provide only criticism of our world, we cannot get any instructions for action out of it and even criteria for criticism are then impossible since they too still belong with the old world which is to be rejected. In other words, radical total criticism blocks the inspiration to action and leaves us stranded, not knowing what to do. Moreover we see – this is the second way – that some of these theologians on the one hand allow radical and total criticism (from which no directives for action emerge) but on the other hand turn for political and social directives to 'the wisdom of this world', social philosophy and ethics, roughly in the way in which Karl Barth did this in his well-known Tambach speech of 1919: the preaching of the kingdom of God is swallowed up in radical criticism of all social and political heritages and systems and is denied if we even dare to put in a hyphen. What must we then do as Christians in the social and political sphere? Choose the best solutions possible, says Barth. So the solution is a kind of doctrine of two kingdoms. We have seen that Moltmann's political theology also does the same thing: the directives which he commends do not come from the cross and resurrection but from general human wisdom: humanitarian principles. But the problem is again that the doctrine of two kingdoms is suspect, not to say excluded, by all theologians who keep to the doctrine of the one Word of God. For this doctrine serves precisely that purpose: to show up all other lords or authorities for what they are and simply keep to the one Lord, Jesus Christ.

Where do we go from there? If theologians do not want a doctrine of two kingdoms because they find it unacceptable and at the same time do not want to leave out directives for social and political action, there is nothing left – here is the third way – but to take these instructions from the future which has not yet been revealed, God's other world. But in order to be able to do that it is necessary to weaken the qualitative difference between the kingdom of God and our kingdoms, the future and the present. If the kingdom of God is so far away that people can never arrive at it or have a share in it then there is no sense in making the coming of the kingdom a criterion for political and social action. That only makes sense if we allow it to make a real contribution, in other words if we can believe that our political and social action is a help towards the coming of the kingdom of God.

This is where the shift comes, naive as it is necessary, when the one Word of God ends up as a social and political promise of the future; instead of being a transcendent entity outside the world the kingdom of God becomes an entity within the world which realizes itself in our history. The Future becomes the future.

Of course this shift does not take place as schematically as I have described it here and it certainly does not happen deliberately. Especially among the theologians who want to stay close to Barth there are a whole series of assurances which at least in theory exclude the possibility that the kingdom of God can come to us through human hands. But anyone who has accepted the role which is given to human action in the matter of the coming of the kingdom of God is up against a dilemma: either our action does not bring it close, in which case we must refrain from holding up the future as a source of inspiration, or we begin from the future and allow it to inspire us to action, but that implies the faith that our action – political and social – paves the way to the kingdom of God.

The latter approach is the easiest. Therefore it does not make much sense – here, at any rate – to investigate which theologians with their outline proclamation are on this side and how far they want to go with it. Moreover a number of them are still so steeped in the problem of political directives – where you get them from and why they are Christian, and so on – that they never, or hardly ever, arrive at an evaluation of the role of political action – what we do with them. The questioning is not yet sharp enough, so the problem has not yet been worked through. What we can say is that many Christians are more or less innocently occupied in making this change. It has become a kind of community theology. Social and political action is evaluated as the way in which and the means whereby the kingdom of God can be established in our world.

That is an enormous revaluation of social and political action: we must be aware of that. We even hear it said that secularization is playing a part in the zeal of believers for collaboration in development, for the Third World, for a change in society and so on. But that is a mistake. Politics and social action are not secularized as in the doctrine of the two kingdoms but rather sacralized, elevated to Christian religion, indeed made the heart of it. That is what I call the socializing of faith. It is just a matter of terminology: I could have also said the politicizing of faith, but socializing goes further and includes more, and with goodwill we can also include political action in it in this chapter. Thus I do not mean secularization, as I have already made clear: Christians are not detached from their faith by social action; at least they themselves do not think so. Far less can we say that in the contrast between 'horizontal' and 'vertical' concern Christians now sadly opt for the horizontal. On the contrary, horizontal *is* vertical; in politics and social criticism doing is what we call religion, faith. Faith and religion do not wither away and disappear but express themselves as political and social action, doing good, intervening for others, and so on. From this perspective we can rather say that faith blossoms. To put it in an evocative way: by the socializing of faith I mean that faith and social action are not two different things, but faith coincides with social action.

I think that it is not a mistake to say that for many Christians this identification has already been made and that there are even more who feel defenceless against it, although they would like things to be different. That is not surprising. A person does not stand alone as an individual but is always in a plurality of social and political relationships which largely make him or her the individual that he or she is. We have been able to see that already in different ways. The concept of the individual would not be significant if there were not a society. It therefore stands to reason that in its outline proclamation the Christian church also has something to say about social and political relationships. It would have a very strange doctrine about living if it did not. Nor is it surprising that in a time of rapid social and political change the church and Christianity should be occupied with the social and political areas of Christian doctrine and seeing whether the premises of Christian faith can contribute anything to social and political reorientation, for example, as we are finding today, in the form of a new theological theory (outline proclamation) for the political and social practice of Christianity. Not only the outside world but also and above all the members of the Christian community themselves can regard this new outline proclamation as a good thing, as a way out of the morass of irrelevance in which church and Christianity threaten to get stuck. Political and social questions are important questions, and we have seen in the first chapters how much people are affected by them. If it can be made clear that these questions are the real questions of faith, or better still the authentic questions of faith, things will be more tense in the church. There will be few people who can avoid the fascination of this concentration of faith on social and political action. Believing is something different from preserving traditional doctrine. That is what we have thought for too long, and therefore in the church the feeling of 'this is not it' has become much too strong. Living faith makes discoveries, needs discoveries and discoveries in turn again invite living faith, even to positions where it cannot really thrive. Such processes are unavoidable and are in no way a hindrance to the continued existence of church and faith, let alone a fatal threat. One can always draw back. Christians should always take note when faith is no longer prospering. That is the time when a reorientation begins.

I think that we have reached that point over the socializing of faith. In the long run it will leave us empty-handed. Moltmann has described the risks run by living faith as a never-ending dilemma between identity and relevance. If the Christian church is only concerned with its identity, it becomes irrelevant; if it seeks only to be relevant to its surroundings then it risks losing its identity. That is also true. In that case we think in terms of church and identity and of course see it as an ideal that the church should be relevant precisely in its identity. What I propose here is meant somewhat more personally. I am not so much thinking of the church – though I find Moltmann's formulation of its dilemma fruitful – as of the faith of the individual. Anyone who limits faith to, or makes it coincide with, social action gets stuck when politics and society do not bring the future which is so vigorously desired and for which there is such hard work. We must have something to offer to people who stand around empty-handed. In that way we can keep ahead of developments. So I shall try to describe what price Christians have to pay for the socializing of faith: they lose something in so one-sided a conception of faith. In putting the losses on one side I shall at the same time be providing a positive formulation of what there is in Christian faith other than social and political commitment and what prove to be unmistakable elements of the industrial or even post-industrial society in which we live. I shall set out below, point by point, as in the previous chapter, the limitations of Christian faith, if we only keep to the doing side of it, the tasks it calls for. When I say faith I am thinking both of faith as trust-and-action, faith that we are doing the right thing, and also of faith as believed faith, the Christian tradition of faith.

1. To keep only to the 'doing' side conflicts with the Christian tradition of faith. That is not in itself a sufficient argument against adopting a new course, though it is worth mentioning, but to be concerned only with action is not in fact a new way: to put it somewhat ambiguously, and deliberately so, it is as old as the way to Rome. It is beyond all question that action must also mean socially orientated action. The poor must be able to earn an honest living, the hungry must be able to look after themselves again, the environment must be watched over and preserved, if future generations are still to have a life, and so on: I am just pointing out what has to be done. Christians act for the well-being of all: that is a natural ingredient of their faith. Believing includes action. But action is not the whole of faith and is not identical with it; far less is it the case that we can further narrow action to politics and social involvement. Of course there has been a good deal of dispute over the relationship between faith and action down the ages: what is the right place for action in the overall framework of faith? The controversy between Rome and the Reformation was for centuries dominated by this dispute. I shall not go deeply into things here, since even in the heat of the strife there was never a party which held that faith was identical with

action. That would be to make our souls and our bliss dependent on our own action, and that is so much in conflict with the character of the Christian message of salvation as grace that we should be denying the Christian tradition altogether if we thought in this direction. That is, unless souls and bliss are a mistake and people are wrong to be concerned about reconciliation with God, the forgiveness of sins and confidence beyond death, because that is not what things are about. That is the case for many Christians today. That need not surprise us, since it is the other side of the socializing of faith.

2. Keeping only the obligations of faith is no new thing. It comes close to the ethicizing of Christianity, and the great example of that is Kant. According to him, believing is obeying the ethical imperative, and in his view you cannot express the seriousness of this imperative other than by seeing it as a command of God. So really God is needed only to endorse the command. Is there such a great difference between Kant's ethicizing of Christianity and today's socializing? At all events the difference does not lie in the way in which God is needed: that is the same in both cases. Kant found Christian doctrine superfluous, where it sought to be more than an indication of the unconditional character of the command-ment (as coming from beyond). It is just the same with the socializing of Christianity. All that many Christians retain of God (often it is all that they have been given) is that intervention for the oppressed, the struggle against discrimination and so on, must come from him, and that you are in the way of the kingdom of God if you throw yourself into this struggle. The seriousness of this commitment is not under discussion, far less am I arguing that 'being in the way of God' is not an authentic religious experience, but – as I have already said – it represents only the obligations posed by Christian faith and that means that it is mistaken: not only in respect of Christian faith itself, which has more in it than obligation and commandment, but also in respect of human existence, which is too precarious an adventure to be coped with through a faith which has only a demanding side.

Let me make that clear with the help of the question why the ethicizing of Kant has taken the form of socializing in our time. I think that the answer is that because of the preference for socialism in political theology, the nineteenth-century belief in progress has come to find a home in Christianity. This belief in progress consists in the view that all the problems of human existence can have a social solution if we do our best and devote ourselves unconditionally to social concerns. Here we see the mistake to which the socializing of faith comes very close. For not all the problems of human existence are of a social nature and for that very reason all cannot have social solutions.

3. Before I take up the thread further, one incidental comment is worth making: to keep only to the active side of faith makes for strict and fanatical believers. For Kant morality was a matter of enormous seriousness. It is still the case that countless people like to see Kant as the philosopher of Protestantism (the Protestantism that is then regarded as strict, Calvinistic faith), and conversely numerous others identify morality with the strict moralism of Kant and therefore would most like a morality without morality. But the socializing of faith is on the same level as Kant's ethicizing of Kant. People only believe that not everything can have a social or political solution if they see that. So they believe that it can have such a solution if we only work together at it. Servitude, injustice, poverty, crime, discrimination – all can be banished from the world if only we believe that they can be. Thus belief in action becomes a strict and even a fanatical belief: anyone who does not join in, who regards such a belief as a mistake and does not think 'the great leap forward' worth the price is regarded as a traitor to the cause and is therefore murdered both literally and spiritually simply for not sharing belief in progress.

4. To return to the line that I was following previously. The socializing of faith implies that Christian faith is left with what others (those who are not Christians) have not done and cannot do. That is a point, but is not why people became Christians. You do not need to be a Christian to be aware of the environment, to support Nicaragua or Afghanistan. It is assumed that Christians are also concerned for such aims, but non-Christians support them just as much. Christian faith would be no longer needed if there were no more to it than action; or, to put it more strongly, if faith is socialized, in the long run it disappears.

So what have we lost? The answer to all these questions and problems which cannot be resolved by society or politics, the questions which are raised by suffering, by death, by the fate that we encounter in what we get and what we do not get, by the impenetrability of the future, by the injustice that we suffer and cannot remove, or that we have done to others and can never make good again: the last and deepest questions of existence. A faith which has nothing to say about them, which leaves us with them because it has nothing to say, is a narrow faith and is not in any position to help people to live. And a church which has nothing to talk about but social and political solutions and views is hardly worth the trouble – even if it does refer to God and his commandments. But the next chapter will be about that.

5. Christian faith – to which people belong through believing as an act of trust – has the answer to the question who God is, whether he does exists, whether his rule – if he does rule, which some ask despairingly – can be just and loving, whether it is meaningful for us to trust, whether it makes sense to open up our lives to God (prayer and intercession) and whether God is (or has) a solution for what we ourselves can no longer repair: the damage done to others. The answer to these and similar questions disappears if faith coincides with social action; indeed the questions no longer arise. That is a colossal impoverishment for faith. Without doubt, as I have already said, Christians also experience God as one who gives commands. But God is not to be experienced only as one who gives commands, as Augustine already knew, but also as a companion. We experience the blessing of his creation, the mysteries of his guidance in our life – what would there be left for us to dispute with God if we could not talk about God's guidance? – and the blessing of reconciliation and security in his eternal concern for us does not come to an end at death. A person must hear more of God than what he or she is to do, if he or she wants to be able to be and remain human. That is what I shall be discussing in the last chapter.

6. Moreover the socializing of faith has a disappointing ending: it offers both the believer and society less than we thought. As a result the life of the believer is impoverished. He or she becomes tired, overwhelmed, out of breath with action since it is never enough. Those who do not become tired of it, become moralists with a superficial existence: the sense that we must *act* is dislocated and is no longer incorporated into the broader experience of God as Creator and Redeemer.

But in that case does society not benefit if Christians socialize their faith? I am not even convinced of that. To regard social salvation as salvation *par excellence* produces illusions which no one can substantiate and gets in the way of all the things that we cannot do or can get down to doing.Precisely because it is a faith, socialized faith leaves behind a great gap, a gap of superficiality which overlooks everything that goes wrong on this side of the grave and is not put right by us. It is the faith of Western people who are doing well and feel that the world has been helped enough if everyone can live freely, without poverty, exploitation and oppression. Certainly we must fight for freedom, for the banishing of poverty and oppression, but that is fighting for well-being, and well-being is not salvation, not even if we give it a religious aura. In that case we make faith a religion of humanity but humanity does not thrive in the optimistic climate of such a faith. More is needed to help people live than to provide a good society and a good life within this society.

7. If Christian faith is narrowed to a doing-faith or is socialized, it becomes just as narrow as if it were not combined with action, including social and political action. Faith works through action.

17. Why the church?

I have taken the title of this chapter from Rudolf Augstein, a German journalist who some years ago wrote an article entitled 'What is the church for?' In it he spoke of the way in which he had been alienated by the shift of accent within the churches: you would expect them to be about God and faith but they were about collaboration in development, political support for Latin American minorities, a more just division of prosperity and the politics of the arms race. Augstein found that suspect: why this interest in things which did not appear on the church's agenda at an earlier time? At a time when the interest of institutions stands and falls by their political relevance, must churches prove that they are still relevant today? Do they want to breathe new life into themselves by being about another, more interesting topic? If that is the case – and Augstein does not doubt that he is right over one or other of these possibilities – we may well ask whether the churches have not outlived themselves. What is the church for if the church only does what others already do, continue to do, better and with more knowledge of things? Augstein's article ends with the proposal that the church should be abolished. It has no useful place on this earth.

It is clear – even from my summary, but the article itself is still clearer – that Augstein is no friend of the churches. So he cannot imagine that the political and social interest of many of the churches and church members is genuine and derives from a deep concern for people who suffer or are disadvantaged. I think that we can underestimate this concern and the fact that the church's political interests began there. And we should be ashamed of our own past in which – as Augstein also points out – churches paid too little attention to the need for political and social changes. Moreover I would explain the wave of political and social concerns within the churches – more favourably than Augstein – as a necessary piece of catching up. Of course such an explanation also gives one the chance to say that for the moment we must regard this phase as now being complete, at least if the churches do not want to change into social or political organizations. For Augstein's main argument – and the title of his piece – is right: why should the church *qua* church primarily do things which are done everywhere else? In the previous chapters I called that duplication, repeating from the church or theology or the sphere of faith what others outside the church and theology have already thought and practised. One example that we have seen is the way in which Karl Barth established democracy on the basis of christology, but at the end of his argument (in *The Christian Community and the Civil Community*) he could not avoid pointing out how remarkable it was that Rousseau had got that far without the gospel.

In the earlier chapters I have already indicated that if the church duplicates what others are doing it virtually halves itself. That is the line I shall be taking in this section.

First let me introduce a practical argument: if the church primarily duplicates what is being done by other authorities, for example engages in welfare work or politics, it must either become a welfare organization or a political party, and thus professionalize itself, or it must accept that people know very well that it is not really professional, that others can do things better and that therefore the church is not needed, not even – indeed precisely not – in those things about which it is showing such concern (though in fact duplicating work). In practice, that happens when churches seek their salvation in a political and social role: the last reason for belonging to the church then disappears. Moreover I am not convinced that the churches lose so many members because they give so little scope for political and social commitment. Rather, we should turn things round and note that when it comes to the novelty of politics in the church, people give up precisely because all there is to be found in the church is what they hear day in and day out in the news, the commentaries, the political propaganda and the statements by action groups. The reason why people go to church, want to belong to the church and indeed want to serve the church is because something other is expected of the church – I should really say something Other – but if their expectations are not fulfilled, their concern disappears. Of course that must also be said in the right quarters. To embellish God with politics does not help the church out of the morass, but takes it back to the Middle Ages, and an autocratic church is even less use. I shall return to this point in this and the next chapter. First I must say a bit more about duplication.

The practical, actual consequence of this is that the church no longer needs to duplicate – in political or social terms – what others are doing. The reason why that is the case – and cannot but be the case – is that the other side of duplicating what others do is halving oneself. That too is only a term – and is open to discussion – but it indicates very honestly what I have in mind and have tried to show in a more academic way in the previous chapters. In its outline proclamation the Christian church has two packets: one it shares more or less with everyone, and that one relates to the wisdom that is needed for us to live (together). This wisdom is one element in Christian proclamation, and it is incorporated into it as coming from God as creator and sustainer. It is Christian and at the same time can be found elsewhere. Alongside that in its proclamation the Christian church has something which is not found elsewhere: the story of Jesus as Christ, as revelation of God, as reconciler and redeemer. Halving means that to the degree that the Christian church seeks its salvation in taking up political and social questions, it drops that which cannot be found elsewhere and cannot be taken over by any other authority. There is only one answer to the question 'Why the church?': because there is something which only the Christian church has and can distribute. In that something – about which I shall say more shortly – lies the reason for its existence and the limit of its concern with politics and social criticism.

In adopting this position I am concentrating the nature of the church on what I see as its real task, the preaching of that about which only it can know. That does not imply leaving other things as they are. Christians are also individual believers: they are members of the church but also members of society, citizens of the two kingdoms, and must also be trained for the kingdom of this world. Throughout the book I have also brought this side of being the church to the fore. But for the knowledge of the wisdom that is needed to live in the worldly kingdom, one need not be a Christian nor does one need the Christian church.

Those who disagree with this must consider whether they are not refusing to accept the secularization process that they were the first to invoke. If by secularization we understand the way in which certain tasks which the church was accustomed to do have become superfluous, the duplication in the sphere of politics and social action can be explained as a later refusal to surrender tasks and have them carried out by a world which is competent to perform them or, if you prefer, which is no less competent than the church. Many tasks have already become secular down the ages: reading and writing, philosophy, sociology, morality. People no longer need the church in these areas to know what they have to know – action is another matter, but that equally applies to church members. So politics and social criticism belong in the same series. The Christian church cannot alter that and set itself up as a guardian or conscience. That would be to put its own existence at risk (by duplicating) and would in any case be impossible (it lacks the competence). But the church is also the authority which can know that things need not be like this. It can be at peace with secular wisdom because it knows that this wisdom – secular though it is – comes from God the creator and sustainer. If it duplicates, then it puts at risk not only its existence but also the reason for that existence: it keeps the wrong half.

The knowledge that we do not share with others – and what non-believers also ask about when necessary – is the *proprium* of the Christian church (something that it alone has): God the creator experienced at the same time as judge, reconciler and redeemer. That is what one generation within the Christian church teaches to the next: it offers a search pattern with the help of which people can set out and encounter God as judgment and acquittal, as blessing and mystery, as hunger and fulfilment, as commandment and companion. The rest is an optional extra: catechizing about collaboration over development, a sermon on nuclear weapons and their threat, a parish evening on homosexuality; but it only presents *within the church* an elucidation of the search pattern in which God can be found. For how collaboration over development can emerge from the grass roots and the best strategy for it is also known by others; whether a nuclear war is threatening and how to avoid it is discussed everywhere (though with controversial conclusions); and how the cake of national prosperity can best be divided is something after everyone's heart. But for the search pattern for God – at least God in terms of the Chrisitan tradition – we can go only to the Christian church. If no more is said there, then there is simply no one who is talking about God, since there is no longer a Christian church.

Why the church? For this reason. Said in all modesty, it is irreplaceable because it has something irreplaceable in it. It is there to bring that to men and women. The worst that the Christian church can do is to run away from its task, out of anxiety that people will find it unimportant when it talks about God. But that idea is based on an illusion, the illusion that the Christian church keeps itself in being by concentrating its outline proclamation on politics and social concern. However, the outline proclamation is much more important. It is a search pattern, with the help of which people may learn to experience God themselves. If the search pattern is not adequate, then they look in places where he is not, or rather, does not allow himself to be found. There is also a place for political and social struggle there: God's sphere lies the other side of politics. That also goes for the place of the Christian church. The church is not dull and stale; it responds to a primal hunger of human beings in so far as God responds to that hunger. I shall return to this in the last chapter. It does so, that is, unless the search pattern is inadequate and people do not encounter God. In that case people are bored to death in the church.

In this way we become clear what the church is for. Of course the dividing lines cannot be as schematic and well considered as I have indicated here. Churches are living communities in which all human experiences and preoccupations must be given consideration, including political and social questions. I cannot imagine any Christian congregation in which at an appropriate time nuclear weapons, ecological questions, the Third World and natural disasters in Africa would not – also – be the theme of a church service. But that need not introduce doubts as to what the outline proclamation of the church is and what it is not. The minister need not always preach about society and politics. We may free him from this burden. It is not his task to understand everything. Nor may he preach on it every Sunday. We must cut off his escape into 'interesting questions'. He may show that God, as the Christian search pattern portrays him, is above all that.

Must the church then give and receive no instructions for living in the midst of all the complications which humanity and society pose to faith? Of course it must. But let us make things a bit clearer.

Who is the church that gives instructions for action in society? It is one generation which hands on a heritage to the next. It almost never succeeds and therefore the process of handing on and instruction is always difficult: a new generation must find its way in a new, different world. The process of tradition can completely block that way. But what kind of instructions does one generation give to the next? They are the guidelines for life in the one kingdom, the worldly kingdom of creation. The church is, as I have shown, increasingly less competent to instruct Christians about that life and thus increasingly more directed towards the experience and the wisdom that living in two kingdoms can provide. Instructions for life in modern society also have a place in the church: if necessary, they can be given from the pulpit. But they are different from the outline proclamation, the message of the gospel. They are in principle instructions which Christians (as citizens of two kingdoms) give to one another, the one generation to the other, the one person to the other. Both theologians and non-theologians can have a role in the process of tradition – which people are is not too important. These, too, are instructions in terms of two kingdoms and that gives a good deal of latitude for different views among Christians. Here Christian freedom has one of its roots: theologians or church leaders who make statements about secular matters are opinion leaders or whatever we like to call them, indispensable in the process of the forming of Christian opinion about life in the world, but not the church. Church people are quite happy to accept the existence of political movements provided these do not speak in the name of the church.

Seen from this perspective the Christian church – as a church – can be much more relaxed about the political struggle and social problems than it is today, without being detached from them. The gospel itself offers us a model that we can live from. Someone came to Jesus with a family dispute. 'Master, tell my brother that he must share the legacy with me.' But Jesus said to him, 'Man, who made me judge or arbiter over you?' (Luke 12.13, etc.). The answer Jesus gave has often caused amazement, but that need not be the case. He is not saying that the question of the legacy is unimportant, but that it is for others, judges and lawyers, to decide. At the same time Jesus indicates that he is concerned with it, but on another level: 'Take heed and beware of all covetousness; for a man's life does not consist in the abundance of his possessions' (v.15). Questions of distribution and political questions must be fought out, but the Christian church is not there for that; the relevant institutions can do it better. Yet the Christian church is not remote from these questions: its outline proclamation implies that a person is more than possessions, that covetousness is not rewarding but evil, and that abundant possessions cannot save a person from death and judgment. Both directives converge in the person of Christ: the political struggle which has to be waged and the relativizing of this struggle through the knowledge that a person is more (and needs more) than politics. Although Christians distil from the gospel directives for action in the life of the secular kingdom, they are judges and arbiters without forgetting that a person does not benefit from gaining the world if he loses his soul.

To sum up, the features of the Christian church are determined by its saving message of God, who makes himself known as creator, reconciler and redeemer; through its instruction, by which it provides a search pattern with the help of which people can find the one whom they sought deliberately or unconsciously; through prayer and intercession for all human beings, especially for those who suffer under the violence of their fellows; through meditation and stillness; through the inward and outward working of love. I deliberately put the last point in these terms. A church without works of love cannot be a church; a church which limits love entirely to politics and no longer sees any place for works of mercy loses its vision. Political service to the neighbour is anonymous service; it can be done by ballot papers and propaganda for a political ideology. That is far too little for the Christian church. Love of neighbour cannot be adequately shown with verbal assurances. It is also a miscalculation, an almost utopian trust in the outcome of the social and political struggle, from which the church will certainly come out damaged. Politics cannot be everything. In fact they amount to very little, necessary though they may be. If the Christian church seeks to practise love of the neighbour only through social and political channels, a very large number of people will never be helped. The diaconal service of the Christian church is one of its most distinctive features.

So the face presented by the Christian church is different from that presented by Christians. Are there then two Christian faces? Yes, that is not only an unavoidable conclusion but also an indication

of the actual situation. The Christian church is not the world's welfare
worker, though welfare work is desperately needed. Christians too
take part in it. Far less is the Christian church a political organization
or an institution which serves to foster social interests, although we
cannot live without such institutions. You can see Christians playing
a role in such institutions and organizations from top to bottom. Or
even more clearly: the question of bread is a primary question for
all human beings, but the Christian church is not the organization
that sees to bread. There are other organizations of bakers. And
again other organizations have been formed for the distribution of
the bread. Christians can be bakers; the church cannot. Christians
are judges and arbiters, but the church has not been appointed for
that. From this point of view the doctrine of the two kingdoms is
not confusing but a healthy principle of order that allows the church
to be the church and the world the world.

18. Here and hereafter

The socializing of faith obscures what faith and the church are about. And how does it help the individual? For in the end everything that we call political and social criticism begins with him or her. The reason why we do not want dictatorships and totalitarian states is because individuals disappear and are removed for political ideals. I think that there are good reasons for an opposed view and for us to end up with the opposite of what we meant by the socializing of faith. What we really want is for everyone to be free of injustice and oppression, since they lead to someone who is summed up by his or her social and political roles and thus gets submerged. I shall devote this last chapter to clarifying such a position.

Karl Marx used the phrase that we must see man as a 'social entity', a complex of social relationships. We came across the expression earlier; here I want to go into it rather more deeply. The definition of being human can be understood from the perspective of Marx's social philosophy. It is meant to be both descriptive and normative (that is also both its attraction and its misfortune): a person is neither more nor other than the sum of his or her relationships and anything else is impossible. So we must think of these relationships exclusively as social relationships, as human roles in the economic process of production. The implication of this description is that the quality of being human depends on the quality of social relationships. How these relationships look in turn depends on the persons involved since they are not natural phenomena but the product of historical human action. Thus a person becomes himself or herself by being the creator of his or her own relationships, and to the degree that individuals improve these relationships they improve themselves.

That sounds hopeful, but reality so far has produced another picture. That happens because Marx overlooks one link: who improves the improvers of social relationships? Unless that is explained, the explanatory theory becomes a circular argument: nothing is explained, but on the basis of an optimistic view of human beings it is asserted that someone improves relationships and thus becomes better himself or herself. The 'better' comes in like a jack-in-the-box or, what in this case amounts to the same thing, it drops down from heaven. The theory of progress fits only if a human being is not just a social whole but more, and the theory of the social entity can only succeed if we leave aside progress. That is what it amounts to.

Now my purpose is not to refute Marx's social philosophy – I would need more space than I have here for that. What I am concerned to do is to bring out the picture of humanity which emerges in it. Let us assume that social conditions constantly improve. Of course the theory does not work out in practice, as I have just shown; a price must be paid for each improvement which in turn puts a question mark against the improvement. The reason why Marx and his successors do not emphasize this price is because they reckon that everything will turn out well in the end: suffering will be forgotten and we shall be in the fatherland. The price is paid in utopian and eschatological terms, something which is only possible if one accepts a hereafter (which Marx eschewed). I shall return to that.

But first let us forget all that, and assume that social relationships really do get better and that therefore human beings get better too. Even then one bridge is not crossed: a person is and remains imprisoned in his or her social roles, if he or she is no more than a social whole. That defines his or her value. That need not mean that individuals become valueless as such; it means that their value can never rise above the value that they have for the collective. To coincide with your social roles means to coincide with your social significance or the significance which you have for the whole. The history of socialism offers touching pictures of people who were ready to apply this description of being human to themselves and to sacrifice themselves for the progress of the workers' movement, but it offers just as many repugnant pictures of the use – or misuse – that the authorities made of this view of humanity. If the value of an individual person is determined by his or her social and/or political significance, then the individual is interchangeable, may be sacrificed to bring in the future and may still be proud to serve as 'dung on the fields of the future' (Henrietta Roland Holst), a future that is offered as a shimmering horizon but one which he or she will never reach. I shall come back to that, too. First let me pick up the thread and say that collective ideas of the future correspond with a view of humanity in which the value of a person is determined by his or her social and political role. If a person is identical with this role, then he or she has no surplus value; the individual is then submerged and becomes interchangeable with others. I hasten to add that this description applies not only to classical socialism – above all inspired by Marx – but also to all collective expectations of the future. The ambitious attempt by Teilhard de Chardin to see humanity as a long history of development towards God suffers from precisely the same fault: the individual no longer counts, but only the collective. That has been shown clearly in the novel *The First Adam* by Boeli van Leeuwen.

How does a person then achieve a 'surplus value' which prevents him from being submerged in his or her social roles? Only religious faith can help there. I have deliberately first put this in general terms because not only Christian faith is in a position to save a person; other religious convictions can also do that. However, from now on I shall be concerned with Christian faith and its significance for the individual in his or her social and political roles. Christian faith preserves a person from coinciding with his or her social roles by giving the individual an independent inalienable relationship, a relationship with God which transcends all other relationships and gives him or her an identity independent of any social and political significance.

This has brought us to the point where we can see that the socializing of faith does not provide the contribution that it expects of itself. That is not so much because of the fact that human beings figure in it as a social whole. It could be, but that would take a separate book to investigate. I do not think that it need be, since I am not claiming that the socialized faith emerges from that picture of humanity but rather that it does not prevent that picture from gaining a firm footing. When faith and social action are identified there is no chance for the image of an independent relationship to God which cannot be reduced to any other; on the contrary, the relationship to God is at its best in the relationship to society.

Here, at least in practice, we have returned to humanity as a social whole; the individual takes on value because and in so far as he or she is an element of society. This value even acquires a religious aura, but that does not prevent the person concerned from being identified with his or her social roles and inevitably also being submerged in them. Only an individual, personal relationship to God can protect someone from that, but as we saw in the previous chapter, in socialized faith nothing is left of this relationship other than that which goes with God's society: a new identity, a new name, an unassailable confidence in God's eternal love are realities which drop out of socialized faith because they are unimportant. So the loose threads of the previous section of this paragraph come together here: the personal relationship with God is the pivot of the Christian outline proclamation; it is something which is sought (and found) in its own right since that is the foundation on which a person can be open to God, and at the same time it is an indispensable part of being an individual in society in so far as it keeps the individual from being identified with his or her social roles. So to this degree we can approve of Karl Barth and his view that the Christian church has all the more social and political significance the more it is itself and preaches the gospel of justification by faith (though I found when I discussed this position that we have to go further than that): faith gives a person an identity which transcends the social and political identity that he or she has as a member of society. I shall not separate these aspects again, but keep them both together for the rest of this dicussion.

1. Christian faith gives individuals identities of their own by attributing a personal relationship with God to them, but it does so in its own way. Eternal salvation from God – as distinct from social well-being – is not collective salvation nor is it realized in a collective way. Of course the Old Testament – which is also part of the Christian tradition, though the Christian church has to read it in a 'Christianized' form to make it that – puts forward the opposite view in some of the oldest layers of its tradition: punishment and salvation are given and experienced collectively. But all that the oldest layers of tradition can offer is what we would call social salvation, God's blessing or well-being: all this takes place this side of the grave. On the other side of the grave there is no salvation, but only forgetting and being forgotten: there is no communication with God and God's salvation can no longer be enjoyed. Moreover – and this is important

– in later layers of the Old Testament we see thinking in collective terms broken through by an outline proclamation in which members of society are reminded of their personal responsibility. They can no longer hide behind or in collectivity, though in that case they are not represented in the government but are expressly held to account by Israel's God for their own actions: 'the soul that sins shall die'. At the same levels of tradition we can see the first trace of an intimation that relations with God are not broken off at death. But we shall be discussing that theme in due course. The process of individualization, as I shall call it from now on, reaches its climax in the Old Testament in the Psalms. A large number of these are individual hymns in which an individual opens his heart to God and expresses all that is in it: joy, sorrow, numberless fears and anxieties, and not least the peace and security that one feels when being aware of the presence of God. For this reason Luther could say that the Gospels and the Psalms are enough to see a Christian through life.

In the New Testament – the *magna carta* of Christian faith – the process of individualization is complete. The preaching of John the Baptist, of Jesus, of Paul (about Jesus) is at the same time a preaching which calls those who hear it to conversion and faith and associates that faith with salvation; indeed in extreme formulations it can even call that faith salvation. All are called to God's salvation, but people enter into it by entrusting themselves to God and God's promises of salvation. That happens because the salvation proclaimed is no longer social salvation, no longer prosperity as the blessing of creation, but God's eternal salvation which extends beyond death. This salvation is not collective, nor do people have a collective share in it.

In this sense one can say that Christian faith individualizes people by bringing them personally to entrust themselves to God and his word of salvation. Without doubt that is reflected in the culture in which the Christian church has become institutionalized religion. Where that faith has a chance, it is no longer so easy to let the individual be submerged in his or her social and political significance. Once people have learned the 'surplus value', they need no longer be Christian to maintain the value of this legacy.

In this view of man – and here I am making a slight digression – there is also a practical test which we can use to assess the acceptability or unacceptability of political régimes within Western culture. Of course that can and must happen by means of a critical examination of the ideology from which they begin: is this consistent? from what picture of man does it begin? and so on. But to reject a theory is not always enough to reject a régime. We are certainly called to do the latter when individuals in the political arena have lost their 'surplus value' over against the collective, as this is indicated in the government, and are used as a purely political means rather than as an end in themselves.

If one cannot believe except as an individual, this individualization nevertheless happens within the Christian faith in a very distinct way. That can become clear to us through a comparison with Buddhism. Where Buddhism presents itself as a religion it stands alongside Christianity: Buddhism, too, individualizes a person and prevents him or her from being taken up and submerged in social roles. But there is a difference, a difference that is also significant in social terms. Christian faith individualizes a person not only by associating him or her as a person with God but at the same time by pointing out the neighbour. That arises out of the character of the God of Christian faith: God is love. One becomes a Christian only as an individual, but one does not remain alone in Christianity.

2. If we go deeper into the content of God's promises of salvation – the *pièce de résistance* of the Christian outline proclamation – a second aspect of personal relations with God develops, an aspect which again in one sense has social significance. God's promises of salvation address human beings entangled in disasters that they have brought upon themselves. In the classical language of faith that means sin. They address human beings who are subject to death: if the material prosperity that a person manages to achieve – and most people do not manage to achieve any – is all there is, what benefit does our toil bring if we cannot share in it? God's promises also tell us that it is impossible for us to order our lives in the world in the way that we know we must. There are sin, death and the law – three powers which we cannot get the better of but from which the Christian message of salvation frees us by allowing us to share in the eternal salvation of God which here in our earthly world offers itself as forgiveness of sins and life in freedom: bad conscience, the fear of death and moral impotence no longer prevail. Anyone who is in Christ is a new creation.

In all modesty the Christian church has to add that people should not have much of an illusion about Christian life as a new creation. But whether Christianity gets something from its own message of salvation or wastes its inheritance, at all events it has an answer to the problem that I put earlier as 'who improves the improvers?' If social relationships make up human beings and human beings make up social relationships, there is no reason to assume that things will go better with human beings and society. The input – to put it in computer terms – determines the output. If the improver is not himself improved, then the conditions which he or she has created cannot be improved. Christian faith is therefore of great significance for society, precisely because it addresses people personally and tells them that something must happen to them. It fills the gap that the belief in progress leaves by making it clear that not only must social relationships be changed but also – and much more fundamentally – people themselves; indeed it also offers a way to this change. According to its own interpretation of itself the Christian church is the community of people who have followed this way and now share in the eternal salvation of God.

The Christian church can only fail to live up to these expectations, and that in fact is what it does. It provides less than we had expected: changed people would live differently with one another. Once that has been said, we must add that 1. it lives its common life as a church community under the conditions of the worldly kingdom and 2. even more, it does not serve as a model for society nor does it form the advance guard of it. The church is not society. It certainly checks society by its way of living in two kingdoms: through Christians and their participation in society and politics. That means 3. that under the conditions in which they live Christians do what they can to realize the well-being of society and at the same time they keep a society alive for more salvation than social well-being can offer.

3. The most fundamental aspect of the personal relationship with God is that a person is given a future which extends beyond death and the grave. That too is personally of great importance for us: it reconciles us to the incomprehensible and bewildering experience of death, but at the same time has far-reaching significance for social and political action. The classical Roman Catholic catechism gave as the answer to the question why a person is on earth: to serve God here and be happy in the hereafter. About 1970 a book by Roman Catholic theologians and essayists appeared under the modest title:

'We should already be happy here on earth' (my translation is somewhat free) and at the time when I am writing many Christians have got beyond that stage and are thinking what so many other people think: if you don't get it here you won't get it elsewhere, as there is nothing else.

In another context I have tried to show that Christian faith becomes quite a different faith if belief in the hereafter vanishes from it. Almost all its doctrines presuppose the hereafter or end up with it in so many words. I need not repeat all that here. Here I shall just stress what is connected with our theme and has some influence (on social and political action). We have already met this connection with our theme in all kinds of forms and in many places. It can be put most simply and most obviously in the form of a question: is social salvation all the salvation that a person may expect? Or in terms of the Roman Catholic catechism: is there only a here and not a hereafter? Don't be put off by the term 'hereafter'. Its purport is to indicate that everything does not end with death but that the grave has another side where God's friendship will again find a person and keep him or her in eternal happiness.

If social salvation is all the salvation that people may expect, only one conclusion is possible: in that case everything must happen here, all happiness must be forged here, all enjoyment enjoyed here and all obligations performed here. For what is not received or done here will not happen anywhere else. It is this unavoidable conclusion which has such colossal social consequences since it brings quite a different perspective to life and action; if we think this perspective through thoroughly we shall find it distasteful. That is already true in general terms. Even someone who does not accept Christian faith will find it difficult. For Christians it is different yet again. The consequences of it are so far-reaching – here I recall that they are the consequences of the socializing of faith – that Christians must go back on their tracks if something is still to be left of faith.

That everything must happen here (I shall use these terms for the sake of brevity) first of all means accepting mercilessness. Human beings have different starts in life: some are gifted and some are not; some are weak and some are strong; some healthy and some sick, and so on; but the gifted, the strong and the healthy have the advantages and the others the disadvantages. What the latter lack cannot be made good; they are saddled with their lot; we may be able to do something to compensate for it but we cannot change it. Much more appalling, because people have more of a hand in it themselves, is the injustice that is done; the injustice that in most cases cannot be made good and more often is not made good. The millions of dead who have been led astray by the authorities, murdered by oppressors, have been used as 'dung on the fields of the future' by those seeking to improve the world or have died of hunger before they could grow up: who or what has a remedy to prevent all that happening? Certainly most people to whom you say that reply that this is precisely the point of their social criticism: that sort of thing must not go on and must be challenged with all our strength. But let us assume that the struggle begins today and that it is carried through successfully – but more about that in a moment – what about the millions from the past who are long dead and buried, who had nothing and never will get anything? Do they no longer count? Must they be written off? Can we write people off for ever? That seems to me to be inconceivable and to go completely against what Christian faith has told us about the value of being human – indeed the value of even one human being. But the struggle is not beginning today, and even when it is begun it will have little success, and even when it does prove successful the outcome will have to be safeguarded by the very means against which the struggle was undertaken: violence and power. 'We can easily cope with that', the slogan of socialized belief, is for this reason first a miscalculation about our own action: if everything has to happen here the executioner continues to triumph over his victims; his advantage even becomes unassailable, it is an eternal advantage.

But that is not the only thing. It also implies an overestimation of our own action. The sense that injustice in the world derives from human beings is not enough. 'We can easily cope with that' forgets that we ourselves are persons and forgets even more the hands that we have dirtied and continue to dirty. It divides the world into 'the good guys' and 'the bad guys' and always puts itself on the side of the good. It is a strange, superficial cowboy Christianity, the other aspect of overestimating oneself. There is nothing to look forward to.

That also applies to its last characteristic, fanaticism. If everything must happen here, it *must*. The world must be different *now*, political action must be carried on by us *now*, and with violence;

there can be no more waiting; postponement of the satisfaction of needs is no longer on: postponement amounts to refusal. This last point makes it clear that the so-called wave of hedonism – I use the term for want of anything better – is not responsible for the decline in Christian faith; on the contrary it is caused by doubts over life after death. The anxiety that everything ends with death makes people consumers who cannot wait any longer, no longer know how to cope with adversity, suffering and death and therefore will not be trend-setters for a new style of life other than 'I'm all right, Jack.'

So far I have talked about the hereafter as a postulate: the price we pay if we leave it out. That is not enough. The question remains whether Christian faith is right to keep the hereafter as a postulate of faith which – in whatever language is used – corresponds to reality. Many Christians now put a large question mark against that, even if they do not want to socialize Christianity (whether they may not yet end up by socializing it is a question that I shall only touch on here). They prefer to point to the Old Testament, where we find this conception only at the periphery. That is right and even important. At all events it shows that religious faith is not necessarily born of anxiety about death. So there is no reason why the conception of a hereafter should have its roots in this anxiety (which all human beings experience). If we are looking for a *Sitz im Leben*, why should it not lie in the feeling that an unjust world needs to be adjusted if we are to be able to breathe in it. Justice is adjustment. Why would it be wrong to believe in a process of adjustment which lasts for ever and why would it be more appropriate to believe in the eternal advantage of the executioner over his victims?

But that is enough; we need not pursue the point further here. Although the idea occurs sporadically in the Old Testament, it is an explicit theme in the New, indeed a theme which becomes explicit in the New Testament and which in the case of Jesus is set against the background of the Old Testament (Luke 20.27-40). For the Christian church the hereafter is a conclusion which follows from the reality of God. He is a God not of the dead but of the living (v.38). The church sees this conclusion confirmed in Jesus' resurrection from the dead. A person does not lose God when he or she dies, since God does not lose this person. Relations with God are eternal because God is eternal. According to the Christian message of salvation, that is the last and most profound purpose of God: he finally keeps him or her for eternity. Whether that is of social and political importance is a question which cannot be raised here. The value of faith is not determined by its social or political significance, no matter what further importance this may have.

Bibliography

H.Berkhof, *200 Jahre Theologie*, Munich 1985

John Cobb Jr, *The Structure of Christian Existence*, Westminster Press, Philadelphia 1967

C.-H.Grenholm, *Christian Social Existence in a Revolutionary Age*, Uppsala 1973

J.Gustafson, *Theology and Ethics*, Oxford University Press 1981

E.Jüngel, *Mit Frieden Staat zu machen. Politische Existence nach Barmen V*, Munich 1984

H.N.Kuitert, 'Dood: einde of nieuw begin', in id., *Lezingen en forumdiscussie 7 April 1984, VUSA centrum Amsterdam 1984*, 3-13

H.M.Kuitert, 'Ook een politiek onbelangrijke kerk moet blijven', in *Moet de kerk zich met politiek bemoeien? Controversen rond het spreken an de kerk. Kahier an het Bezinnungscentrum 6*, ed. A.W.Musschenga and W.Haan, VU uitgeverij 1985, 17-34

W.Pannenberg, *Anthropology in Theological Perspective*, Westminster Press and T.&.T.Clark 1985

K.Popper, 'Utopia and Violence', in *Conjectures and Refutations*, Routledge and Kegan Paul 1965

A.Rich, *Radikalität und Rechtsstaatlichkeit*, Zurich 1978

D.Rossler, *Die Vernunft der Religion*, Munich 1976

N.Schellhaas, *De politieke theologie van H.Gollwitzer*, Kampen 1984

E.Schillebeeckx, *Christ*, SCM Press and Crossroad Publishing Company 1980

C.Schmitt, *Politische Theologie*, Leipzig ²1934

D.Sölle, *Politische Theologie*, Stuttgart 1977